Living God's Word
One Scripture at a Time
An Encouraging Personal Perspective

Judy Arnold

Living God's Word... One Scripture at a Time
Judy Arnold

Copyright © Judy Arnold
Published By Parables
October, 2018

All Rights Reserved. No part of this book may be reproduced or utilized in any form or by any means, electronic or mechanical, including photocopying, recording, or by any information storage and retrieval system, without permission in writing from the author.

ISBN 978-1-945698-76-7
Printed in the United States of America

Readers should be aware that Internet Web sites offered as citations and/or sources for further information may have been changed or disappeared between the time this was written and the time it is read.

Living God's Word
One Scripture at a Time
An Encouraging Personal Perspective

Judy Arnold

About the Author

Judy Arnold is a lifelong resident of Sulphur, La. She loves the Lord and wants to share her personal encouraging perspective about The Word- one Scripture at a time. In her life, she has had the hand of God touch her in so many awesome ways and feels she should share those moments to encourage others.

In her first book: A Miracle Healing Surviving Fungal Meningitis, she shared the miraculous healing of her husband. A man literally at deaths door and how God brought him back healed and whole. In this new book, she shares the miracles in her own life through Scripture with her personal perspective in various life situations. She hopes this book will help others live a victorious life in Jesus!

Judy Arnold

Dedication

This book is dedicated first to the Lord, My Father and my best friend.

Without him in my life, I wouldn't be here today sharing the Word through Scriptures. Second I want to thank Jennifer for giving me a chance to share my personal perspectives of living the Scriptures one day at a time.

She trusted my love for the Lord and her own reputation in letting me read the word and add my observations and life experiences. I pray my book will not only encourage people but motivate them to read the word more fervently and receive all the blessings God has for them. It has opened my eyes and my heart more to understand just how God loves a sinner like me!

Word Summary

(A)
Accountability Adoration

(B)
Be a Doer
Believe
Be Still
Be At Rest
Bitterness
Blessings
Blessings in Obedience Boldness

(C)
Chaos
Choice
Chosen
Comforter
Consequences Cornerstone

(D)
Diligent
Doing What's Right
Do Not Fear
Doubt

(E)
Edification
End of Days
Endurance
Establish
Eternity
Exceedingly

(F)
Faithfulness
Fearless
Fruit of the Spirit

(G)
Give Thanks
Glorify
God's Love
Good
Gossip
Grace
Great and
Greatly to be praised

(H)
Haughty Eyes
Healing
Helpmate
His Wonderful Deeds
Holy-I Am
Holy Spirit
Honor
Hope
How great is Our God

(I)
I called-He heard
Immanuel
Impossible
Inside
Integrity
Inner Beauty

(J)
Joy-Not Happiness
Jehovah Jireh
Jehovah Nissi- Jehovah Raah
Just and Judge

(L)
Light of the World
Lost and Found
Love

(M)
Make a Joyful Noise
Malice
Mercy
Mighty
Miracles
My Rock, My Refuge, My Strength

(N)
Nature

(O)
Omnipotent and Messiah
Omniscient and Omnipresent
One

(P)
Peace through Faith
Perfect Love and Mercy
Perfect Peace
Prince of Peace and Prophet
Promises
Prosperity
Purpose of Grace
Putting God First

(R)
Rebellion
Redeemer
Redeemed
Remember
Refuge and Blessing
Rejoice
Refuge
Respect
Restoration
Righteous Living
Risen Lord and My Rock

(S)
Sanctification
Savior
Saved
Self- Absorbed
Sing
Storms in Our Lives
Sovereign
Speak Up
Strength
Stronghold
Strong in the Lord
Strong and Courageous
Submit

(T)
The Lord –My Strength, My Peace and My Everything
The Spoken Word
Truthful and Wickedness
The Way, the Truth and the Life
The Lamb of God
The Whole Will of God
Transcendent and Wise the Name of God

(U)
Unto the Lord
Unconditional

(V)
Victorious

(W)
Walk Humbly
Witness

(Y)
Yield to God

Judy Arnold

Living God's Word... One Scripture at a Time

Word of the Day - Accountability

This Scripture is the foreshadowing of end times when we will all be judged and held accountable for our "works" here on earth. What we did with what we were given "our gift", if you will that God gave us to further His kingdom and help bring the lost to the knowledge of Salvation in Jesus Christ.

Did we bury our gift inside or hide it afraid to use it or did we use it to the fullness of our being as God intended? I use to struggle with this very thing. I was always asking God what it was he had for me to do, what my "gift" was. I am blessed with being organized to the point of being OCD but I could not see how that could lead someone to Christ. So I kept praying and asked God what he wanted me to do. I love talking to people, listening to their problems and would immediately know what Godly advice to give them, praying that it would help in some way. My nickname was Dear Abby. But again it didn't seem like the gift God wanted me to use and I became frustrated. It seemed so insignificant to me. I was just listening, consoling and praying with them. No great thing in my eyes. But a good friend said to me one day, don't you see what you are blessed with? The gift of discernment. I had to literally look it up and it totally stunned me. I had been using my gift and I didn't even realize it! I was just doing what came natural to me. It was an eye opener for me and gave me joy and peace!

God has a plan for each of us, a gift to use for his glory and if you just seek him and ask him, he will reveal it to you! When he does, use it with all your might! Shine your light in this dark world so others can see Jesus in you and through you! Show them the joy and peace in your life through Salvation in Jesus and help bring lost souls into the kingdom of God. Time is shorter than you think and when you stand before the Lord don't you want to hear, "Well done, good and faithful servant"? I know I do!! God bless you all!

Matthew 25:23-30 New International Version (NIV)

23 "His master replied, 'well done, good and faithful servant! You have been faithful with a few things; I will put you in charge of many things. Come and share your master's happiness!' 24 "Then the man who had received one bag of gold came. 'Master,' he said, 'I knew that you are a hard man, harvesting where you have not sown and gathering where you have not scattered seed. 25 So I was afraid and went out and hid your gold in the ground. See, here is what belongs to you.' 26 His master replied, 'you wicked, lazy servant! So you knew that I harvest where I have not sown and gather where I have not scattered seed? 27 Well then, you should have put my money on deposit with the bankers, so that when I returned I would have received it back with interest. 28 so take the bag of gold from him and give it to the one who has ten Bags. 29 for whoever has will be given more, and they will have an abundance. Whoever does not have, even what they have will be taken from them. 30 and throw that worthless servant outside, into the darkness, where there will be weeping and gnashing of teeth.'

Word of the Day - Adoration

How can we not adore our heavenly father? After everything He has done for us yet we are too lazy or too busy to stop for one minute to love on our Merciful God? Shame on us!

We are so quick to offer up a prayer when we are in trouble and need a Miracle. All of a sudden he is the most-important person in the world. Yet we can't seem to muster up even 5 minutes to love on our heavenly Father!

I am as guilty as the next person some days. I go all day long taking care of issues in my live and fall into bed. Most of the time I fall asleep praying and never finish. Usually waking up later in the night, asking for forgiveness. Our family, friends or coworkers, nothing in our lives is more important as our Lord. We need to get on our face and give glory, honor and adoration to the one who gives us forgiveness, mercy, grace but most important our salvation! Our eternity in heaven!! Adore the one true Living God! Give his praise and love on him!!!

Isaiah 6:3
   And one called out to another and said, "Holy, Holy, Holy, is the LORD of Hosts, the whole earth is full of His glory."

Deuteronomy 13:4
   "You shall follow the LORD your God and fear Him; and you shall keep His Commandments, listen to His voice, serve Him, and cling to Him.

Judy Arnold

Word of the Day - Be A Doer!

To hear the word and not do it leads to deception, but to hear the word and do it leads to blessing. How many times do we hear an awesome teaching at church, something that just gets in our spirit that's just for us? A" prompting" from God to do something and we know it? My first thought is usually that's for me and I need to do that. Then I leave church, get busy with life and don't follow through. That is disobedience plain and simple yet we use excuses like "I forgot" or I got too busy. The word of God is like a mirror that reveals to us the very thoughts and intentions of our hearts. It shows all our ugliness, our pride, our self-centeredness, all the things that hinder us from blessings in our life. But, if we just take a quick glance at the word once in a rare while and rush out the door, without doing anything to address the problems that it reveals, it won't do us any good.

Let's concentrate on hearing the word of God and trying our very best to listen and be a DOER!!! God bless you all today in everything you put your hands to. We are blessed and highly favored of The Lord!

James 1:22-25 English Standard Version (ESV)
  22 But be doers of the word, and not hearers only, deceiving yourselves. 23 For if anyone is a hearer of the word and not a doer, he is like a man who looks intently at his natural face in a mirror. 24 For he looks at himself and goes away and at once forgets what he was like. 25 But the one who looks into the perfect law, the law of liberty, and perseveres, being no hearer who forgets but a doer who acts, he will be blessed in his doing.

Romans 2:13
  For it is not the hearers of the law who are righteous before God, but the doers of the law who will be justified.

Word of the Day - Believe

I have had so many people say they believe in God in some way or the other, but do they really? Most people who say that have God in a box. They take him out when they have-a problem. Or they put him in the back of their minds bringing him out only in time of trouble.

But that's not what God wants from us. It's so easy for us for to cry to him for help in times of distress but what about the rest? I believe in Jesus, his death, burial and resurrection not just because the Bible says it. I believe because I have seen miracles, healing, impossible things answered with prayers and even my husband being brought from the brink of death. But even those awesome things aren't the only reason although are they are great miracles none the less.

I believe because I know that I know that I know that Jesus died for me so I could have life-eternal life with the Father in heaven! Through his suffering I was made whole and Righteous in my Fathers eyes by His RIGHTEOUSNESS! Do I believe? Yes with my whole being, am I sure? Yes with no doubt whatsoever. So with your mouths and hearts and soul, lift up Jesus, our savior, praise him with everything in you and most important. Believe in him with all you might and give praise to the King of Kings and Lord of Lords!!!

John 3:12-15 New International Version (NIV)
> 12 I have spoken to you of earthly things and you do not believe; how then will you believe if I speak of heavenly things? 13 No one has ever gone into heaven except the one who came from heaven - the Son of Man. 14 Just as Moses lifted up the snake in the wilderness, so the Son of Man must be lifted up, 15 that everyone who believes may have eternal life in him."

Judy Arnold

Word of the Day-"Be Still"

It's so like God to bless me on my first day with my favorite two Scriptures. So that being said, let's see exactly what being still means. In Greek it literally means "hush. Webster's Definition is-to be quiet, calm, to have peace. If you are like me, the chaos in your life keeps you in constant turmoil and being still is the hardest thing to do. I pray for things but I never sit still long enough for God to reveal his answer. Instead I try to fix it or constantly worry about it. When we stick our hands in trying to do Gods job things usually get messed up.

Trusting in the Lord in the middle of what seems like an impossible situation takes strength and faith but we have that kind of faith within us. We just have to surrender to God and know that he ALWAYS has us in the palm of His hand. Next time you are in mess that causes you to fear, worry, or be anxious over, remember this-. Jesus calmed a raging storm for the apostles with just three words Peace be still! He is with you and will calm the storms in your life and give you peace if you will trust Him and just BE STILL! I pray you all have a blessed peaceful day in the Lord!

Psalm37:7
> Be still before the Lord and wait patiently for him; do not fret when people succeed in their ways, when they carry out their wicked schemes.

Psalm 46:10-11
> 10 He says, "Be still, and know that I am God; I will be exalted among the nations, I will be exalted in the earth."11The Lord Almighty is with us; The God of Jacob is our fortress.

Word of the Day - "Be at rest in the Lord"

What a powerful statement! Isn't it awesome that no matter the situation or circumstances we have a resting place, a safe place to run to in hard times and trouble? Rest in the arms of a loving God that calls you friend, his child, his creation- made in his Image. The image of Christ that should reflect in our daily lives - to be Christ- like. God Knows and sees all our troubles! Rest in the knowledge of who God is, who you are in him and remember God loves you unconditionally!!

Matthew 11:28 (ASV)
  Come unto me, all ye that labor and are heavy laden, and I will give you rest.

Isaiah 40:31
  But those who hope in the LORD will renew their strength. They will soar on wings like Eagles; they will run and not grow weary, they will walk and not be faint.

Word of the Day - Bitterness

To forgive someone is one of the most difficult things to do in your life. Especially if they never apologize, its takes real strength to forgive them. The hardest thing for me has been forgiving myself for all the regrettable mistakes I made in my younger adult life.

Things that make me cringe when I think about them. Many nights of tears and praying for forgiveness until God opened my eyes to the word. Knowing what Jesus did for me, a sinner, the mercy and forgiveness I received from him turned my heart and life around. Holding bitterness in your life for any reason quenches your spirit, hurts your heart and keeps you from the joy God has for you! Let it go, forgive and live in peace!

Hebrews 12:15.
"See to it that no one comes short of the grace of God; that no root of Bitterness springing up causing trouble, and by it may be defiled."

Ephesians 4: 31-32
"Let all bitterness and wrath and anger and clamor and slander be put away from you, along with all malice. Be kind to one another, tender-hearted, forgiving each other, just as God in Christ also has forgiven you

Living God's Word... One Scripture at a Time
Word of the Day - Blessings

Sometimes we get so busy and caught up in everyday life we miss the smallest blessings. Things other people call luck or coincidence when Blessings come their way. If we would just slow down and "smell the roses" as we have always heard, we would see the hand of God in the simplest things. Everybody notices big blessings but the small ones evade us because we're not focused on God. Every lost your cell phone or misplaced your keys- how many of you get frantic and search everywhere instead of asking God to help? You would be surprised how quick he answers because he wants to bless us. Every been in a hurry and ran to Walmart only to find the parking lot full but turn the corner and there is a parking space right in front by the door? That's a blessing but how many of us stop and thank God for that?

I've had people say well That's just luck and in a way I guess that's true- I'm "lucky" that I have a Father that loves me So much that he would do such a simple thing to help me. We need to pay less attention to this chaotic world and more to the everyday blessings we miss .Isn't it a blessing to have a God we can run to, confide in, pour our heart out to, trusting him with every aspect of our life?

Our refuge not just in times of trouble but in every instance of our lives. It's my peace and comfort knowing the Lord is my refuge, my strength, my blessing and all I'll ever need or want in this world. Eternity with our Father in heaven is a blessing I cherish and look forward to when my race here on earth is finished!

Psalm 46:1-3
  God is our refuge and strength, a very present help in trouble."

Psalm 18:2
  The LORD is my rock and my fortress and my deliverer, My God, my rock, in whom I take Refuge; My shield and the horn of

my salvation, my stronghold. "But blessed is the one who trusts in the Lord, whose confidence is in him? They will be like a tree planted by the water that sends out its roots by the stream. It does not fear when heat comes; its leaves are always green. It has no worries in a year of drought never fails to bear fruit

Living God's Word... One Scripture at a Time

Word of the Day - Blessings in Obedience

Do you have that "Special place" to go to worship God and give thanks for all your Blessings? A church home where you feel safe, uplifted, trusted and loved? A place where you aren't judged by what you wear, or by your social or financial status? That place you feel the presence of God when you walk through the doors? That peaceful place to give your offering to God and give thanks for everything has done?

God wants us to fellowship and spend time with other Christians, to lift up each other in Prayer, to rejoice in each other's blessings and give God the honor his deserves through our tithes and offerings. By obeying his word in these things, he blesses everything we put our hands to, making our lives a living testimony of his goodness and grace! I hear so many People fuss about churches asking for tithes and offering but I look at it as obeying Gods Word, giving back what is already his and watching him enrich my life with overflowing blessings and peace. But ultimately my reward is eternity in heaven with Jesus and that my Friends is something I look forward to every day! Peace and blessings in the Lord

Deuteronomy 12:4-7 New International Version (NIV)
 4 You must not worship the LORD your God in their way.5 but you are to seek the place the Lord your God will choose from among all your tribes to put his Name there for his dwelling. To that place you must go; 6 there bring your burnt offerings and sacrifices, your tithes and special gifts, what you have vowed to give and your freewill offerings, and the firstborn of your herds and flocks.7 There, in the presence of the LORD your God, you and your families shall eat and shall rejoice in everything you have put your hand to, because The LORD your God has blessed you.

Judy Arnold

Word of the Day - Boldness

Sometimes it seems like a hardship to be bold in situations where speaking out against something you know is wrong. That boldness is Doing God's will no matter what people say or think of you. You know that God is always on your side when you are bold so you don't have to be afraid. Sometimes when I'm riding in my car listening to Christian music, singing and praising God, I know people probably think lm a-little crazy but I don't care. We need to have courage to be bold, to go against the grain so to speak, to do the right thing no what the consequences. Be bold for God, Stand up and honor God in all your do! He has you in his hands always!!

Hebrews 4:16
   So let us keep on coming boldly to the throne of grace, so that we may obtain mercy and find grace to help us in our time of need

Psalm 138:3
   On the day I called, you answered me; you made me Bold with strength in my soul.

Word of the Day - Chaos

Definition of Chaos—A state of complete disorder or confusion. So many people have chaos in their life which leads to trouble with their Children, trouble in relationships and in their life in general. We have so much going on at one time, that we don't have time to even think. What happen to families sitting down at the table eating supper together? Or sitting around the living room playing games as a family or the most important thing is actually talking to each other.

There is no communication between husband and wives, parents and children or even between friends. Living a chaotic life has no peace and eventually ends in destruction. We need to slow down, sit down and have peaceful restful quiet times to think, hear and see what the Lord is speaking to us.

There is so much "noise" that it's deafening at times. So take one night and don't plan anything! No TV, IPods, cell phones- nothing to distract you. Pull your family close, read the word together and actually listen to God. You will be surprised the peace in your spirit and life you will find if you shut out the chaos.

Philippians 4:6-7
"Do not be anxious about anything, but in everything, by prayer and petition, with thanksgiving, present your requests to God. And the peace of God, which transcends all understanding, will guard your hearts and your minds in Christ Jesus

Ephesians 2:14
"For He Himself is our peace

Judy Arnold
Word of the Day - Choice

Life is... really all about the choices we make and how they shape our lives. Most people I know tend to make choices on the emotional aspect of the situation. Me, being one of them which has caused me much grief in my life. I have always carried my "feelings" on my sleeve, letting my emotions control me instead of the opposite. I use to take everything personal, assuming the worst about people. I lost a lot of friends and relationships because of it. Until one day, God showed me through the word how to not take things to heart. No matter what people said or did to me, it didn't really matter. I came to realize that what he thought about me was all that was really important. I've made mistakes in my life because of wrong choices and had to face the consequences. God wants only well for us but gives us free will to make the decisions. What we do with that choice determines the blessings and curses we end up with. By making the choice to follow the Lord, to keep his commandments and live by the word, your life will be as the Lord intended- Full of love, joy, peace and eventually eternity with him! That my ultimate goal and await that day with longing and joy!

Proverbs 3:5-6 ESV
> Trust in the Lord with all your heart, and do not lean on your own understanding. In all your ways acknowledge him, and he will make straight your paths.

Deuteronomy 30:19 ESV
> I call heaven and earth to witness against you today, that I have set before your life and death, blessing and curse. Therefore choose life, that you and your offspring may live,

Word of the Day - Chosen

Can you imagine that you are chosen of God? That he looked down and saw you and chose YOU!! Can you just fathom a Fathers love so deep that He would send his son to die for YOU? So you could be forgiven and free? To live on this earth as a man to experience all the things we go through... hurt, ridicule, rejection, pain, suffering and ultimately death so He could understand how we feel? Can you imagine anyone caring so much for you and wanting a relationship with you that he would sacrifice so much for you? That's exactly what he did. God our heavenly Father did all that for YOU. He chose YOU. Remember when you feel like no one cares, God does and he never ever leaves us. I'm so blessed to know him and its privilege and blessing that I am a "CHOSEN" child of God

1 Peter 2:9 ESV
 But you are a chosen race, a royal priesthood, a holy nation, a people for his own possession that you may proclaim the Excellency's of him who called you out of darkness into his marvelous light.

Jeremiah 1:5 ESV
 "Before I formed you in the womb I knew you, and before you were born I consecrated you; I appointed you a prophet to the nations."

Judy Arnold

Word of the Day - Comforter

Who is our comforter? Jesus told his disciples when he was leaving to go be with Father that he would send a comforter for them. Smith's Bible dictionary defines comforter as (John 14:16) the name given by Christ to the Holy Spirit. The original word is Paraclete, and means first Advocate, a defender, helper, strengthener, as well as comforter. The Holy Spirit lives within us, guides us and warns us of impending trouble, comforts us in times of hurt and distress, and is an intercessor and consoler. He teaches us to pray when the words won't come. He is the voice in our head saying no to sin, and He is that thumb on the back of your head when stubbornness stops you from doing the right thing. What a blessing it is to know that that he lives in us!!! Be blessed in everything you do today!

2 Corinthians 1:3-4
   Praise be to the God and Father of our Lord Jesus Christ, the Father of compassion and the God of all comfort, who comforts us in all our troubles, so that we can comfort those in any trouble with the comfort we ourselves receive from God.

Matthew 5:4
   Blessed are those who mourn, for they will be comforted.

Word of the Day - Consequences- the law of Reaping and Sowing

There are so many instances in the word where God shows us the consequences of our actions whether they are good or bad. He shows us the right thing to do but gives us a choice to decide for ourselves. Jesus came so we could have joy that only He can give, peace beyond our understanding, forgiveness and abundant life. The Bible is very specific about the law of reaping and sowing and the consequences of sin in our lives. Of course God wants us to choose life, for us to be whole and free from the clutches of sin!

But this chaotic world, full of evil tries to pull us down, tell us we are ok without God, unaccountable for what we do. Not so, for the word says the wages of sin are death. Death of our spirit man which hurts our relationship with the Lord. On the internet, TV and everyday life we are bombarded with negativity. This world wants us to think God is dead and we no longer need him in our lives.

We have to turn a deaf ear to the garbage this old world spews at us and remember WHO is really in control. God is still on the throne. He rules and reigns on this earth and in heaven. We are his children and He is our God! Nothing anyone can do or say can ever change that. We have to trust God, keep our eyes on him and not the lies of Satan.

Proverbs 14:29-30 New International Version (NIV)
  29 whoever is patient has great understanding, but one who is quick tempered displays folly. 30 A heart at peace gives life to the body, but envy rots the bones.

Proverbs 12:21
  No harm befalls the righteous, but the wicked are filled with trouble.

Judy Arnold

Word of the Day - Cornerstone and Deliverer

Who is your rock, the cornerstone in your life? Who helps you in every situation, goes before you to make a way in an impossible situation? Who delivers you from the fiery darts of the enemy when you feel surrounded on all sides? Who walks through the fire with you? Who heals you when the doctors give you no hope? Who can you lean on, go to and trust with your whole life and being? JESUS!!!

The one who suffered and died on that old rugged cross that saved and redeemed you, that took you out of that darkness into the light of his glory! The way maker, our deliverer, our savior, the prince of peace, Emmanuel, the Kings of King and Lord of Lords!!! How blessed we are to be kids of the king, made in Gods image, loved unconditionally, made holy and righteous through his sacrifice! Stand up and praise him for He is worthy to be praised!!!

Ephesians 2:19~22 New King James Version (NKJV)
Christ Our Cornerstone
19 Now, therefore, you are no longer strangers and foreigners, but fellow citizens with the saints and members of the household of God, 20 having been built on the foundation of the apostles and prophets, Jesus Christ Himself being the chief cornerstone, 21 in whom the whole building, being fitted together, grows into a holy temple in the Lord, 22 in whom you also are being built together for a dwelling place of God in the Spirit.

Psalm 40:16-17 English Standard Version
But may all who seek you rejoice and be glad in you; may those who love your salvation say continually, "Great is the LORD!" As for me, I am poor and needy, but the Lord takes thought for me. You are my help and my deliverer; do not delay, 0 my God!

Word of the Day - Diligent

di|~i-gent. Adjective having or showing care and conscientiousness in one's work or duties. Are we diligent in everything we do in our daily lives, in the way we treat each other and in the way we serve God?

Conscience -is the personality trait of being careful, or vigilant. Are we careful how we talk to someone showing love and understanding? Are we vigilant in spending time with God? This Scripture describes the kind of lives we should live and the consequences of doing wrong.

In this chaotic world where God is being taken out of everything, where kids are disrespectful to their parents, where elderly people are mistreated and pushed aside, where law enforcement officers are abused, mistreated and blamed for just doing their job, where our president is ridiculed and called mentally ill, we need to be diligent in serving God and remembering who is in control!

1 Peter 5:8 New International Version
  Be alert and of sober mind. Your enemy the devil prowls around like a roaring lion looking for someone to devour. Satan might have power and control over this world but doesn't have power or control over the children of God!

Colossians 3:17 New International Version
  And whatever you do, whether in word or deed, do it all in the name of the Lord Jesus, giving thanks to God the Father through him. Be diligent in all you do, showing care and faithfulness to our loving Father. In all things giving thanks and praise.

Judy Arnold

Word of the Day - Doing what's right

In the "old" days there was a distinct line - black and white when it came to right and wrong. Today people have make their own rules on that subject and the line has become blurred. Now it depends on how each person sees it whether it's right of wrong. When I'm making a decision I don't much care what the world thinks. I judge my actions by what the word says. How does God see it and what does he think about it? Everybody laughs now at the Saying "what would Jesus do" or WWJD but that's exactly what you should do.

My first and only priority is what God thinks about the situation and handle it according to the word. You can find Scriptures on anything you are struggling with and what God thinks and not what you feel. In today's Scripture it gives ways of how you should treat and deal with people. Don't act like you know EVERYTHING, be honest, and live peaceful. Don't try to get back at someone for any reason and help people. If you live according to what the Bible says then you wl always be right with God. Take a little time out of your busy day and spend time reading God's word. It will refresh you and give you a better understanding of how to do what's right in Gods eyes .Have a blessed day in the Lord!

Galatians 6:9
"And let us not grow weary of doing good, for in due season we will reap, if we Do not give up."

Acts 10:38
How God anointed Jesus of Nazareth with the Holy Spirit and with power. He went about doing good and healing all who were oppressed by the devil, for God was with him."

Word of the Day - Do not fear

How many times during our busy day do we worry about one thing or another? Or do we say- I'm scared or afraid this might happen or that might happen? Yet why do we do that when the Bible tells us "Do not fear" 365 times— one for every day of the year. Listen to what the Lord says... "Do not fear, for I have redeemed you; I have summoned you by name; you are mine! "Can you let that sink into your spirit for a minute? God says we are redeemed, he calls us by our name and we are his!! His love and protection surrounds us daily, he walks with us every step we take. We are never alone or forsaken so why should we fear?

Satan tries moment by moment to throw things our way to distract us and get our eyes off God but what he doesn't understand is that no matter what he tries to do, God NEVER has His eyes off of us!!! How wonderful that is! Whenever you start to get anxious, worried or Fearful about anything, think on this... With God by our side, fear has no place in our life!!! God bless you

Psalm 34:4
  I sought the Lord, and he answered me; he delivered me from all my fears.

Psalm 27:1
  The lord is my light and my salvation- whom shall I fear? The Lord is the stronghold of my |life—of whom shall I be afraid?

Judy Arnold

Word of the Day - Doubt

So many things in our lives cause us to doubt God and if he even exist. We tend to blame God when things don't go our way or turn out bad. We doubt Gods goodness, if he hears and answers prayers or even cares about us.

Doubt - a feeling of uncertainty or lack of conviction

Uncertainty causes disbelief and makes our faith waver in God. We are in good company as doubters though. Thomas doubted Jesus was resurrected— can you imagine asking our savior to put your hand in his side to prove your doubt?

Every time something goes wrong, Satan is like a little parrot sitting on our shoulder telling us things like... "See God didn't answer your prayer, he doesn't care about you". Or "If God loves you so much then why did he let this happen?" He wants us to doubt God, to take our eyes off of him just long enough for Satan to pull your life apart! Don't let him, stand on the word and what you know is true. God is faithful, He never leaves us and only has well for us!

John 20:27 (NIV)
Then he [Jesus] said to Thomas, "Put your finger here; see my hands. Reach out your hand and put it into my side. Stop doubting and believe." Even Peter doubted when Jesus called him to walk on the water. The second he saw the wind he was afraid and he began to sink and cried out for Jesus.

Matthew 14:31 (ESV)
Jesus immediately reached out his hand and took hold of him, saying to him, "Oh you of little faith, why did you doubt?" He did but we as believers have to have ultimate faith in the word, in Gods promises and remember that He NEVER LIES. Satan has a way of putting doubt in our hearts and minds, keeping us from the blessings God has stored up for us.

Word of the Day - Edification

Noun. Edification (plural edifications) the act of edifying, or the state of Being edified; a building up, especially in a moral, emotional, or spiritual Sense; moral, intellectual, or spiritual improvement; through encouragement and instruction.

So many people go to church because they think have to fulfill an obligation to God to be in right standing. But it's not just that. It's a place where we go to be with other Godly people, to give praise and to worship Our Lord and to be filled with his word. Sometimes it's the only place some people have peace and feel love. A place where they can be built up and ready to face whatever they are going through.

As fellow brothers and sisters in Christ we should edify each other, sharing with each other spiritually in hope and faith, ministering to each Other in love. Church isn't a building and you can have church anywhere but it's the body of Christ. As Christians we need to meet to encourage and build each other up, praising the Lord in one voice!

Proverbs 27:17 ESV
  Iron sharpens iron, and one man sharpens another

Hebrews 10:23-25 English Standard Version (ESV)
  23 Let us hold fast the confession of our hope without wavering, for him who promised is faithful. 24 And let us consider how to stir up one Another to love and good works, 25 not neglecting to meet together, as is the habit of some, but encouraging one another, and all the more as you

Judy Arnold

Word of the Day: Endurance - Finish the race!

Do you ever feel like you can't go another day dealing with whatever situation you are going through or just life in general? Do you feel weak in your body, mind or spirit and have thought... I just can't do this alone? Well I've got good news for you—YOU DON'T HAVE TO! God is our help, our answer, our stronghold and our strength! He holds us up when we can't take another step, he picks us up when we stumble, and he makes a way where there isn't one. When things just seem impossible, hopeless and you want to give up, remember who you are—a child of God, an heir, made in Gods image, the king's son or daughter.

Lean on the one who put the stars in the heavens, that made the sun and moon to shine and remember HE IS OUR STRENGTH, our peace in the storm and our answer when life seems impossible-Our Father. He has started something good in us and isn't finished yet. Stay strong, finish this race! He is always a prayer away!

Hebrews 12:1—3
> Therefore, since we are surrounded by such a great cloud of witnesses, let us throw off everything that hinders and the sin that so easily entangles. And let us run with perseverance the race marked out for us, fixing our eyes on Jesus, the pioneer and perfecter of faith. For the joy set before him he endured the cross, scorning its shame, and sat down at the right hand of the throne of God. Consider him who endured such opposition from sinners, so that you will not grow weary and lose heart.

Colossians 1:10-11
> So that you may live a life worthy of the Lord and please him in every way: bearing fruit in every good work, growing in the knowledge of God, being strengthened with all power according to his glorious might so that you may have great endurance and patience.

Word of the Day - End of Days

Nobody wants to talk about end of days but it's coming much sooner than most people realize. Are you ready? Are you where you need to be with your relationship with God? So many people tell me they don't have time to be a Christian or that it's just too hard. Or one day when they finish doing what they want to accomplish then they will give their life to God. The word says that we aren't promised tomorrow so waiting until later doesn't seem like a very smart option to me. Tomorrow may be too late. The Bible speaks of a time to come when there will be a great shaking which will cause many to be humbled. Nothing is more important than living for Jesus, totally surrendering everything in your life to him. This Scripture talks about a great shaking of this world and who remains will be the ones who cannot be shaken—the children of the highest God.

Where will you be when the shaking is over? One of the ones who falls away or the one who cannot be shaken? Sold out to God or living for the world? It's your free will to choose your path — choose wisely for there won't be a second chance. As for me, I want to spend eternity with Jesus and awaiting the day when we will be forever with him!!!

Hebrews 12:25-28 New International Version (NIV)
25 See to it that you do not refuse him who speaks. If they did not escape when they refused him who warned them on earth, how much less will we, if we turn away from him who warns us from heaven? 26 At that time his voice shook the earth, but now he has promised, "Once more I will shake not only the earth but also the heavens." 27 The words "once more" indicate the removing of what can be shaken—that is, created things- so that what cannot be shaken may remain. 28 Therefore, since we are receiving a kingdom that cannot be shaken, let us be thankful, and so worship God acceptably with reverence and awe,

2 Peter 3:10

But the day of the Lord will come as a thief in the night, in which the heavens will pass away with a great noise, and the elements will melt with fervent heat; both the earth and the works that are in it will be burned up.

Living God's Word... One Scripture at a Time

Word of the Day – Establish

What does it mean to be established in the Lord? To have an everlasting foundation, a stability nothing in this world can shake, knowledge, wisdom, to stand when things seems overwhelming and impossible. Being established in the Lord is our eternal salvation

Whom will also confirm you to the end, blameless in the day of our Lord Jesus Christ? We walk in the light, sons and daughters of the King. Redeemed, forgiven and blessed of the Lord. Cherish this as you share the good news of Our Lord Jesus Christ and know that we are loved by the Maker of the heavens and earth, Lord of the Universe, God Almighty

1 Thessalonians 3:13
 So that He may establish your hearts without blame in holiness before our God and Father at the coming of our Lord Jesus with all His saints.

1 Peter 5:10
 After you have suffered for a little while, the God of all grace, who called you to His eternal glory in Christ, will Himself perfect, confirm, strengthen and establish you.

Judy Arnold

Word of the Day - Eternity

Eternity—infinite or unending time

Forever is a strong, scary word for some people. But it's a reality in our lives as we won't live forever and where we spend eternity is literally our choice! I don't know about you but spending eternity in hell doesn't sound too appealing to me. Time is short and the decisions we make determines where our eternity is. Forever in the presence of our Savior is something I long for and await the day the Lord either calls me home or takes me home in the rapture. Either way, my home, my eternity is in Heaven forever praising the Lord! How about you.

John 5:24
> Verily, verily, I say unto you, He that heareth my word, and believeth on him that sent me, hath everlasting life, and shall not come into condemnation; but is passed from death unto life.

Romans 6:23
> For the wages of sin [is] death; but the gift of God [is] eternal life through Jesus

Living God's Word... One Scripture at a Time

Word of the Day - Exceedingly, Abundant, immeasurable

Exceedingly - extremely, to a great extent
Abundant - plentiful
Immeasurably - immensely

This is a short but powerful Scripture that reminds us just how big our God is and how he wants to bless our lives in a big way. Sometimes when we have a need, we go to God in prayer telling him what we need and how He can fix it. Our own idea of how it should go or be. But God has so much more for us than we can imagine. Like our earthly father that feels joy from blessing his children with gifts, our Father in heaven wants to give us good gifts too.

To give us joy and happiness in our lives, peace in our hearts and healing in our bodies. He knows what we need before we ask. But he loves the relationship with us and wants us to come to him with our struggles of everyday life. His spirit lives in us and through the Holy Spirit, guards our lives and knows our every thought. Keep your mind and heart focused on God and trust him in All things and he will give the desires of your heart according to His will for your life, .more exceedingly, abundantly and immeasurable- more than you can ever imagine or hope for. You are a child of the King!!! How awesome is that! Be blessed!

Ephesians 3:20
  Now to Him who is able to do exceedingly abundantly above all that we ask or think, According to the power that works in us.

2 Corinthians 928 New International Version
  And God is able to bless you abundantly, so that in all things at all times, having all that you need, you will abound in every good work.

Judy Arnold

Word of the Day - Faithfulness

What has God entrusted you with in your life? Is it the gift of preaching or teaching? Singing or the ability to help people in need? Is it just being a good listener even if you can't really help? We are all blessed with one "gift" Or another but are we faithful to use it as God intended? Or do we stuff it aside because we don't have time? It doesn't matter how insignificant you think your gift is, it's important to God and he wants you to use it to bless other people, to further his kingdom and bring others to salvation! Open your eyes and your heart and see what gift God has given you and use it with a joyful heart. Not only to bless other people but to bless Gods heart and show him how very much you appreciate and love him! Glory and honor to the one who reigns in Heaven and on earth!! Praise His Holy Name!!!

God is both faithful and loving, those who believe in God need to exhibit faithfulness and steadfast love in their lives. How faithful are we to God? God isn't looking for perfect people. But he is looking for people who love him, keep his word and are faithful in their daily walk. How much time do we actually spend having a personal relationship with the Lord? It's not about reading your Bible for hours or quoting '100 Scriptures although those are good things. It's about our personal one on one time we spend with him, loving on him, giving him the praise and honor he so richly deserves.

Sharing our day, our joy and our sorrow with him, talking to our father with a trusting faithful heart. That's the kind of Relationship he desires with us. Take a few minutes today to acknowledge him, talk to him, thank him for your many blessings, let him know how much he means to your life and just how much your truly love him. That will definitely put a smile on your Fathers face and bless you tremendously in the process!

Proverbs 3:3 New International Version
Let love and faithfulness never leave you; bind them around your neck, write them on the tablet of your heart.

2 Chronicles 16:9
"For the eyes of the Lord run to and fro throughout the whole earth, to show Himself strong on behalf of those whose heart is loyal to Him."

Judy Arnold

Word of the Day - Fearless

What does it mean to be fearless? To be unafraid, brave, bold...courageous is my favorite description. Having the courage in every situation no matter how bad it seems knowing that God is in control. Knowing He always has our "backs" and trusting him to do what's best for us. He is our defender, our healer, our very present help in our time of need. Trusting and knowing He NEVER leaves us. My favorite song is The God of angel armies. The words of the song touches my soul. Look it up and listen to the words. That pretty much says it. God is with us always. Have a blessed day in the Lord!

Isaiah 41:10
> Fear not, for I am with you; be not dismayed, for I am your God; I will strengthen you, I will help you, I will uphold you with my righteous right hand.

1 John 41:18
> There is no fear in love, but perfect love casts out fear. For fear has to do with punishment, and whoever fears has not been perfected in love.

Living God's Word... One Scripture at a Time

Word of the Day - Fruit of the Spirit

In today's verse the Lord instructs us what not do, how to treat one another, not be foolish, argumentative or resentful. Sometimes I struggle with those things especially when I've been hurt or used. I love Gods word because he gives us instructions on how to handle any situation that arises. When I feel like I don't know how to handle certain people, I remember the fruit of the spirit and it reminds me of how God wants us to act and live daily.

"But the fruit of the Spirit is love, joy, peace, forbearance, kindness, goodness, faithfulness, gentleness and self—control|." Sounds like a big order but every one of things makes us who we are in God- all these things are what a Christian is and how they should live their life. Can you imagine what kind of world this would be if everyone walked in the fruit of the spirit and treated each other accordingly?

Today as you go about you busy schedule, try to take a minute to treat every person you come in contact with by applying Gods word with love, joy, peace, forbearance, kindness, goodness, faithfulness, gentleness and self-control. You will make them have a better day and in turn you will be blessed!!!

John 15:1-8
"I am the true vine, and My Father is the vinedresser. "Every branch in me that does not bear fruit, He takes away; and every branch that bears fruit, He prunes it so that it may bear more fruit. "You are already clean because of the word which I have spoken to you.

Galatians 5:22-23
But the fruit of the Spirit is love, joy, peace, patience, kindness, goodness, faithfulness, gentleness, self—control; against such things there is no law. Now those who belong to Christ Jesus have crucified the flesh with its passions and desires.

Judy Arnold

Words of the Day.-Give Thanks!

Do you ever just thank God for all the good things He has done for you? Just talking to your Father like you would your best friend? I try to make it a make it a habit every morning, during the day and every night to thank God for the many things he has done for me...strength, peace, joy, forgiveness, mercy, healing and the most important one salvation. In our daily lives we have so much to be thankful for— our spouse, children, grandchildren, and our health. Even small things like a parking space right by the door at Walmart or finding that lost cell phone or keys. God cares about everything concerning our lives and if we just surrender to him and give HIM our life, you will see the total difference it makes! Take time to reflect on what God has done for you and give him than

Isaiah 12:1-6 English Standard Version (ESV)
The Lord Is My Strength and My Song
12 You will say in that day: "1 will give thanks to you, O Lord, for though you were angry with me, your anger turned away, that you might comfort me. 2 "Behold, God is my salvation; I will trust, and will not be afraid; for the Lord God is my strength and my song, and he has become my salvation." 3 With joy you will draw water from the wells of salvation. 4 And you will say in that day: "Give thanks to the Lord, call upon his name, make known his deeds among the peoples, and proclaim that his name is exalted. 5 "Sing praises to the Lord, for he has done gloriously; let this be made known in all the earth. 6 Shout, and sing for joy, 0 inhabitant of Zion, for great in your midst is the Holy One of Israel."

1 Chronicles 16:34
Give thanks to the Lord, for he is good; his love endures forever.

Word of the Day - Glorify

These Scriptures show us the goodness, mercy and the hope we have in God. So many reasons to give him glory, to lift him up and give him the praise he so richly deserves. There are so many instances in the word telling us to glorify our heavenly Father but sending his Son to die for our sins and putting us back in right relationship with him is enough for me. We can glorify him by the way we live our lives and be a witness to the lost.

Our attitudes, the way we talk and treat people shows the light of Jesus in our hearts and glorifies God. So let the light of Jesus shine in you and through your life. Your actions and your words glorifying the Father in heaven. Let your joy in the Lord be so evident in everything you do so people will see Jesus through you, desire to have that joy, bring lost souls to salvation and the Father be glorified.

1 Corinthians 6:20 English Standard Version (ESV)
20 for you were bought with a price. So glorify God in your body

Psalm 86:12 English Standard Version (ESV)
12 I give thanks to you, O Lord my God, with my whole heart, and I will glorify your name forever.

Judy Arnold

Word of the Day - God's Love

For us is unconditional, unchangeable, and everlasting. What a loving God we have that loves us much that he sacrificed his only son so that our Sins could be forgiven and we could be free!! His for us is unconditional, unchangeable, and everlasting. That's real love from an awesome God! Spend time with him today and thank him for a love compared to no other that he freely gives to those who seek him. Hugs to all and hope your weekend is full of peace and joy in the Lord

2 John 4:16
So we have come to know and to believe the love that God has for us. God is love, and whoever abides in love abides in God, and God abides in him.

Psalm 36:7
How precious is your unfailing love, O God!

Living God's Word... One Scripture at a Time

Word of the Day - Good

Today's Scripture describes God in such a way that if we only read the first sentence, it's enough. Psalms 34:8...Taste and see that the Lord is good blessed is the one who takes refuge in him...it reminds me of my favorite saying. God is good all the time and all the time God is good!! Anyone know what Christian movies it's said in? It also reminds me of a Christian song now out called "You're a good, good Father".

Both those statements are true no matter what situation or storm you may be going through. God is good and a good Father and most days I wonder how people that don't know his goodness even survive. We are indeed blessed to take refuge in him and know that anytime, anywhere, he is there for us. A shelter in the storm, a shoulder to cry on, a much needed hug. Our heavenly Father loves us, His children so deep and unconditionally and his goodness and mercy are ours always. Rest in that thought today and know you are LOVED!!

Romans 8:38-39
 37 For I am convinced that neither death nor life, neither angels nor demons, neither the present nor the future, nor any powers, 39 neither height nor depth, nor anything else in all creation, will be able to separate us from the love of God that is in Christ Jesus out Lord.

Psalm 34:4-5 Good News Translation (GNT)
 In Praise of God's Goodness 4 I will always thank the LORD; I will never stop praising him. I will praise him for what he has done; may all who are oppressed listen and be glad! Proclaim with me the Lord's greatness; let us praise his name together! 5 I prayed to the LORD, and he answered me; he freed me from all my fears. The oppressed look to him and are glad; they will never be disappointed. The helpless call to him, and he answers; he saves them from all their troubles. His angel guards those who honor the LORD and rescues them from danger.

Judy Arnold

Word of the Day: Gossip

Gossip, such an ugly word in itself. People do it more often than you realize and cause more damage they will ever know. Gossip break hearts and sometimes ruins lives that can't be repaired. Most people that gossip do it to get attention or a reaction out of the person they are telling.

I think talking about a person behind their back is the most inexcusable thing someone could do. A lot of the time the gossiper wants the person they are talking about to know. So they tell their best friends knowing it will get back to them. These kinds of things hurt to your inner being- to your soul. A soul wound is hard to overcome and destroys people lives. It has happen in my own family and believe me it hurts. So I think people need to think of consequences, the hurt and potential damage they can do to person before opening their mouths with hurtful word

Proverbs 20:19
  Says, "A gossip betrays a confidence; so avoid anyone who talks too much." Words are powerful. They can build up or destroy."

Proverbs 26:22
  The words of a gossip are like choice morsels; they go down to the inmost Parts.

Word of the Day - Grace

Grace it just happens to be my favorite blessing of all, unmerited favor. Something we don't deserve but giving freely from our good father. The number for grace in the Bible is 5 and when I'm going through a storm I see 5, 55 or 555 everywhere I go. A reminder from God his grace is sufficient for me. I love that song, you are a Good. Good Father, that's who you are and we are loved by you, that's who we are!!!! He teaches and guides us, gives us good knowledge and grace to handle anything this world throws at us! I don't know how many times during the day I see his hand in my life and know without his grace and intervention. I wouldn't make it through a single thing! Thank you Lord for our many blessings, your patience with us and giving us your grace and goodness we don't deserve but truly blessed to receive!

Ephesians 2:8 ESV
  For by grace you have been saved through faith. And this is not your own doing; it is the gift of grace.

Titus 2:12 ESV
  For the grace of God has appeared, bringing salvation for all people.

Judy Arnold

Word of the Day - Great and greatly to be praised!

How often do you praise God? Most people think that the only time we praise and worship God is at church. But I say we should praise Him continually not just for what he has done for us but what he does for us on a daily basis. Little things most of us don't even realize. How many times have you pulled in Walmart in a hurry and tired and found a parking spot right up front? Or standing in a long checkout line and a cashier opens a new lane and motions you over? Or buying something you need but can't really afford then at checkout find its 50% off just today.

Do you see Gods hand in these instances? Most people don't and that's the sad part. These little blessings are missed yet so important to God. He loves us that much and deserves to be praised. Even when things aren't going great we should still praise and lift him up in gratitude

Isaiah 12:1-6
Songs of Praise
12 In that day you will say: "I will praise you, LORD. Although you were angry with me, your anger has turned away and you have comforted me. 2 Surely God is my salvation; I will trust and not be afraid. The LORD, the LORD himself, is my strength' and my defense; he has become my salvation." 3 With joy you will draw water from the wells of salvation. 4 In that day you will say: "Give praise to the LORD, proclaim his name; make known among the nations what he has done, and proclaim that his name is exalted. 5 Sing to the Lord, for he has done glorious things; let this be known to all the world. 6 Shout aloud and sing joy, people of Zion, for great is the Holy One of Israel among you."

Psalm 145:3
Great is the Lord and most worthy of praise; his greatness no one can fathom.

Word of the Day - Haughty Eyes

Question: "What does the Bible mean when it speaks against haughty eyes?"

Merriam-Webster defines it as "blatantly and disdainfully proud." The Word is used in the Bible in the evil sense of "arrogant, disdainful and putting yourself above others"; it is often used as being opposite of being humble. Pride is never good and can destroy friendships and the best of relationships. The Bible calls it sin! To have haughty eyes is to have an arrogant demeanor; it's an overall attitude of your heart that causes you or ''look down on'' others. This kind of haughty person puts himself above others, and most disheartening above God!

When we act haughty, we think we are the center of our universe; everything revolves around us. There is usually no concern for what others think or feel and the worse thing, has no consideration for the will of God. Pride, haughtiness ultimately leads to destruction. Cutting us off like a dead tree from the true vine that sustains us. When God is not the center of our world, nothing good can become of our lives. Something to think about!!

Proverbs 21:4
  Haughty eyes and a proud heart, the lamp of the wicked, is sin.

Proverbs 16:18 New International Version (NIV)
  18 Pride goes before destruction, a haughty spirit before a fall.

Judy Arnold

Word of the Day - Healing

We have so many problems these days. Our many health issues, chaos in our emotions, bitterness from hurt than can literally destroy not only our lives but our relationship with God as well. The Lord has a solution in his word for each of these things and so much more. Satan loves to intrude into our lives in any way possible keeping us distracted and our eyes off God... and he's pretty darn good at it. We live in a fallen, evil world where disease is destroying our bodies- but God has healing in his hands for us. Satan tries to destroy our emotions by causing chaos and hurtful things- but God has peace for us!

Exodus 15:26
  26 "For I am the Lord who heals you."

Psalm 147:3
  3 He heals the brokenhearted and bandages their wound

Word of the Day - Helpmate

I so love this Scripture. I don't know about everyone else but I know in my marriage especially that being the helpmate to my husband isn't a job to me but a privilege! I've heard it said that everyone has a soulmate and I know God has blessed me with mine. God made women for men but not to be maids or slaves to them but to be a blessing. God made us to be tender, loving, caring individuals that can be tough as nails and handle any situation put in front of us with Gods help. We can multitask without blinking an eye, yet sooth a crying child with a touch and melt her Husband's heart with a smile.

Genesis 2:18 New International Version (NIV)
18 The Lord God said, ''It is not good for the man to be alone. I will make a helper suitable for him."

Genesis 2:22-24 New International Version (NIV)
22 Then the Lord God made a woman from the rib he had taken out of the man, and he brought her to the man. 23 the man said, "This is now bone of my bones and flesh of my flesh; she shall be called 'woman,' for she was taken out of man." 24 That is why a man leaves his father and mother and is united to his wife, and they become one flesh

Judy Arnold

Word of the Day - His wonderful deeds".

We are so busy in our lives today that I think we forget about all the "wonderful deeds" God has done for us. The ultimate one in sending His son Jesus, to die for our sins, was enough yet he continues to bless us on a daily basis. His mercy, compassion, and forgiveness are gifts we don't deserve yet he gives them freely. He heals our bodies and minds, blesses our finances, and gives us wisdom in difficult decisions. So many wonderful deeds to be thankful for.

Proverbs 21:21
   He who pursues righteousness and loyalty finds life, righteousness and Honor

Psalm 40: New International Version
   Many, LORD my God, are the wonders you have done, the things you planned for us. None can compare with you; were I to speak and tell of your deeds, they would be too many to declare.

Word of the Day - Holy I AM

As I read these Scriptures and the description of the angels with eyes everywhere it makes me realize just how amazing and holy our God is! Can you imagine seeing something like that? It would a little scary. .If you think about all he made, it's overwhelming yet the thought that he made US in his image shows how much he loves us.

The beauty of this earth-the stars, mountains, oceans and the simplest tiny butterfly shows the mighty power and love our Holy Father! I love the story of the burning bush when Abraham asked God who he should tell the people who sent him and God said "Tell them, ''I AM'' Wow. What a powerful yet simple Statement! He was, is and ever shall be! Our God reigns forever and ever and one day we will bow before him praising his name and shouting "Holy, Holy, Holy is the Lord God Almighty! What a glorious day that will be!!!!

Romans 8:26-30 American Standard Version (ASV)
26 And in like manner the Spirit also helpeth our infirmity: for we know not how to pray as we ought; but the Spirit himself maketh intercession for us with groaning's which cannot be Uttered; 27 and he that searcheth the hearts knoweth what is the mind of the Spirit, because he maketh intercession for the saints according to the will of God. 28 And we know that to them that love God all things work together for good, even to them that are called according to his purpose. 29 For whom he foreknew, he also foreordained to be conformed to the image of his Son that he might be the firstborn among many brethren: 30 and whom he foreordained, them he also called: and whom he called, them he also justified: and whom he justified, them he also glorified.

1 Peter 1:16
Because it is written, "YOU SHALL BE HOLY, FOR I AM HOLY."

Judy Arnold

Word of the Day - HOLY SPIRIT

Today's word is the Holy Spirt. Who is the Holy Spirit? He is our comforter, our counselor, He intercedes for us, and he shows us the truth and teaches us how to live. He leads us and convicts us of ungodly actions and thoughts prompting us to live by the word of God. So many times in anger or frustration I want to lash out at the person causing me pain or grief. But The Holy Spirit "thumps" me on the head as I always say and stops me in my tracks. He shows me the correct way to handle difficult situations—Godly ways instead of in the flesh.

I always say he checks my attitude before I end up messing up and making a bad mistake. If you are guided by the Spirit as you live your life for God the best you can, the fruit of the Spirit will be evident in your life. The fruit of the spirit is love, joy, peace, patience, kindness, goodness, faithfulness, gentleness and self-control. I'm still a work in progress but I'm living for the Lord and doing my best!! Be blessed everyone!

John 15:5
> I am the vine, ye [are] the branches: He that abideth in me, and I in him, the same bringeth forth much fruit: for without me ye can do nothing.

Romans 8:26-30 American Standard Version (ASV)
> 26 And in like manner the Spirit also helpeth our infirmity: for we know not how to pray as we ought; but the Spirit himself maketh intercession for us with groaning's which cannot be Uttered; 27 and he that searcheth the hearts knoweth what is the mind of the Spirit, because he maketh intercession for the saints according to the will of God. 28 And we know that to them that love God all things work together for good, even to them that are called according to his purpose. 29 For whom he foreknew, he also foreordained to be conformed to the image of his Son that he might be the firstborn among many brethren: 30 and whom he foreordained, them he also called: and whom he called, them he also justified: and whom he justified, them he also glorified.

Word of the Day - Honor

Do we honor God, really? Do we do everything to the best of our ability to honor God? Or do we do it for our own benefit to receive honor for ourselves? When things turn out for our good do we thank and honor God for the blessings in our life? So many times we pat ourselves on the back, taking the all the praise for our accomplishments. Not once thinking that God orders your steps, going before you and opens doors and removing obstacles in your way! Do we honor God with our bodies, living healthy and clean and taking care of ourselves? Not likely most of the time. I am just as guilty as the rest, not eating right, exercising or getting enough sleep. We live as we want and praying to God when we get sick, overweight and overtired. Do we honor our parents?

Do we listen to their counsel or advice, realizing they have lived through things and have more wisdom than we could ever know? All of these things are in the word, things that honor God by the way we live, love and honor each other and in turn honor God. The one that deserves honor for everything in our lives, past, present and future! Remember, you're every thought, every action, every decision you make should honor our Holy God!!!

1 Corinthians 10:31
  Whether, then, you eat or drink or whatever you do, do all to the glory of God.

1 Corinthians 6:20
  You were bought with a price. Therefore honor God with your bodies.

Judy Arnold

Word of the Day - Hope

What is your hope placed in? This world and what it has to offer, money, possessions, friends? These are all things that will fade away and offer nothing. Our hope should be in the Lamb of God, Jesus our Savior, Deliverer, Our very present hope in time of need. He promises us eternal life in heaven, unconditional love. The world promises happiness which fades but Jesus promised us joy unspeakable and peace beyond understanding. !! Things, friends are temporary but Jesus is forever! Which kind of hope will you choose?? Choose Jesus, choose life!!!

Isaiah 40:31
> 31 but those who hope in the LORD will renew their strength. They will soar on wings like eagles; they will run and not grow weary, they will walk and not be faint.

Jeremiah 29:11 ESV
> For I know the plans I have for you, declares the Lord, plans for welfare and not for evil, to give you a future and a hope.

Living God's Word... One Scripture at a Time
Word of the Day - How Great is our God!!

This brings to mind the awesome song we sing in church all the time!

The splendor of the King, clothed in majesty
Let all the earth rejoice
All the earth rejoice
He wraps himself in Light, and darkness tries to hide
And trembles at His voice
Trembles at His voice
How great is our God, sing with me?
How great is our God, and all will see

How great, how great is our God
Age to age He stands
And time is in His hands
Beginning and the end
Beginning and the end
The Godhead Three in One
Father Spirit Son
The Lion and the Lamb

That says it all— He is mighty, powerful but compassionate, forgiving, merciful and loves us beyond anything our human minds can comprehend. But God demonstrates his own love for us in this: While we were still sinners, Christ died for us. That's enough for me! Although I've had so many miracles in my life that I'm thankful for, my salvation is what has changed me and my life and gives me eternity with my savior- who could want anything more than that!!

Romans 528 New International Version
  But God demonstrates his own love for us in this: While we were still sinners, Christ died for US.

  1 Chronicles 29:11

"Yours, O Lord, is the greatness and the power and the glory and the victory and the majesty, indeed everything that is in the heavens and the earth; Yours is the dominion, O Lord, and You exalt Yourself as head over all.

Word of the Day - Humility

Being humble, a problem so many of us struggle with on a daily basis. What does being humble really mean? I don't think I ever really understood the real meaning of that word. Me, a sinner, living my life as I pleased, ignoring Gods plan for me to have eternal life. Until one day, a bad situation brought me to my knees and I could do was look up! I humbled myself to the Lord and well the rest, as they say, is history!

God in his ultimate wisdom, mercy and grace picked me up and gave me a new life and a hope of eternity in heaven. The above Scripture is a mountain of truth, each verse showing us if we live for God, trust with all our hearts and humble ourselves before him, He will direct our paths. Just give God a chance to show you his plan for your life and the love in his heart he so freely gives!

Psalm 147:5-7
> 5. Great is our Lord and mighty in power: his understanding has no limit. 6. The Lord sustains the humble but casts the wicked to the ground. 7. Sing to the Lord with grateful praise: make music to our God on the harp.

James 4:7 NKJV
> Therefore submit to God. Resist the devil and he will flee from you 8.Draw near to God and He will draw near to you. Cleanse your hands, you sinners; and purify your hearts, you doubleminded. 9. Lament and mourn and weep! Let your laughter be turned to mourning and your joy to gloom. 10 Humble yourselves in the sight of the Lord, and He will lift you up.

Judy Arnold

Word of the Day - I called- He heard.

This is one of the most assuring Scriptures in the Bible to me. Knowing our loving Father is only a call or cry away gives me peace and security in my life. So many people let us down when we need them most and it's disheartening but the Lord never does. He knows what we need before we ask. But our asking pleases God because that's the relationship he wants with us. Knowing we trust him enough to go to him, to cry out to him in our times of trouble, knowing he hears and is taking care of it. My comfort is knowing he is making a way like only he can do. What a blessing to have a Father that loves us unconditionally and will never leave us. Remember to trust God in all things, love him with all your heart and surrender your life to him completely. Then you will know true joy that nothing in this world can take away!! Be blessed in the Lord today!!

Psalm 18:6
   6 In my distress I called upon the Lord; to my God I cried for help. From his temple he heard my voice, and my cry to him reached his ears.

Psalm 34:4
   I sought the Lord, and he answered me: he delivered me from all my fears.

Living God's Word... One Scripture at a Time

Word of the Day - Immanuel,

Immutable |immutable— unchanging

Emmanuel - God with us. Can you just imagine or comprehend a Father that loves sinners like us so much that he sent his son to be born of the flesh? To be able to understand what we go through- our hurts, emotions, trials and temptations. Jesus sacrificed everything for us so we could have eternity in heaven with the Father. I can't imagine the amazement and awe the apostles must have felt to see and experience walking with Jesus! Immanuel-God with us. They got to see it firsthand but we also have him with us in our hearts and spirit—he walks with us through everything!

We are never alone and he never leaves us. Immutable... our God is unchanging, the same yesterday, today and forever! He is faithful and true, he never lies and longs for the intimate one on one relationship with each one of us- his children. As Christmas day approaches celebrating the birth of Our Lord Jesus Christ, the King of Kings, Our Savior, remember why he came, why he lived and why he died that horrible death on the cross! It was for me and for you to redeem us, restore us to salvation and put us back in right standing with the Lord! How blessed we are, righteous by HIS righteousness, born again into the kingdom of God, heirs to the throne and eternity in heaven forever!!! Praise the Lord! A child is born - Immanuel! Christ our King! Hallelujah!

Psalm 102:25-28English Standard Version (ESV)
25 Of old you laid the foundation of the earth, and the heavens are the work of your hands.26 they will perish, but you will remain; they will all wear out like a garment. You will change them like a robe, and they will pass away,27 but you are the same, and your years have no end.28 The children of your servants shall dwell secure; their offspring shall be established before you.

Isaiah 7:10-14 English Standard Version (ESV)

The Sign of Immanuel

10 Again the Lord spoke to Ahaz: 11 "Ask a sign of the Lord your God; let it be deep as Sheol or high as heaven." 12 But Ahaz said, "I will not ask, and I will not put the Lord to the test." 13 And he said, "Hear then, 0 house of David! Is it too little for you to weary men, that you weary my God also? 14 Therefore the Lord himself will give you a sign. Behold, the virgin shall conceive and bear a son, and shall call his name Emmanuel.

Living God's Word... One Scripture at a Time

Word of the Day - Impossible

What a discouraging word that is used by so many people in times of trial and trouble. Things go bad then worse and then most people say... well it's just impossible! Well I say... They must not know our God!!! Because I know "all things are possible through Christ who gives us strength!! People tend to speak things out of their mouth in situations that seem hopeless, only making matters worse!

Faith as small as a mustard seed— that's tiny yet enough to move mountains in our way!! There is no situation too big for our God if we only trust in his word, have faith in every trial and tribulations and believe. We tend to be our own worst enemy at times. But if we keep our eyes on the Lord, there is nothing he won't do for us. He is faithful to us and never ever late! Seek him, believe in him, trust him in all things and watch what blessings he has for you!!

Matthew 21:19-22 New International Version (NIV)

19 Seeing a fig tree by the road, he went up to it but found nothing on it except leaves. Then he said to it, "May you never bear fruit again!" Immediately the tree withered. 20 when the disciples saw this, they were amazed. "How did the fig tree wither so quickly?" they asked. 21 Jesus replied, "Truly I tell you, if you have faith and do not doubt, not only can you do what was done to the fig tree, but also you can say to this mountain, 'Go, throw yourself into the sea,' and it will be done. 22 If you believe, you will receive whatever you ask for in prayer."

Judy Arnold

Word of the Day - Inside

The Bible says "fear not" 365 times once for each day of the year. I wonder why he reminds us in his word every day not to be fearful. It's in our human nature to have fear or to be afraid. I think if we are honest with each other, every one of us has been afraid or fearful sometime in our lives. But it's ok because HIS Spirit lives INSIDE us. We have HIS power, His love, His strength and self-control inside us to help us in times of trouble, hardships, loss and the many things we endure on this earth. Jesus said we would do all the things he did and so much more! Let that sink in a moment

Timothy 1:7 English Standard Version (ESV)
 7 for God gave us a spirit not of fear but of power and love and self-control.

2 Timothy 4:16-18 English Standard Version (ESV)
 16 At my first defense no one came to stand by me, but all deserted me. May it not be charged against them! 17 But the Lord stood by me and strengthened me, so that through me the message might be fully proclaimed and all the Gentiles might hear it. So I was rescued from the lion's mouth. 18 The Lord will rescue me from every evil deed and bring me safely into his heavenly kingdom. To him be the glory forever and ever. Amen.

Word of the Day - Integrity

I absolutely love proverbs. Everything we do has a cause and effect. Every action has a consequence whether it be evil or good, wrong or right. In this Scripture it shows us what is right and wrong and the consequence of each. God shows us throughout the Bible what his will is and gives us a choice of which path to take. But also warns us what happens if we choose our own way. Integrity-the quality of being honest and having strong moral principles; moral uprightness.

Proverbs 10:9-11 New International Version (NIV)
9 Whoever walks in integrity walks securely, but whoever takes crooked paths will be found out. 10 Whoever winks maliciously causes grief, and a chattering fool comes to ruin. 11 The mouth of the righteous is a fountain of life, but the mouth of the wicked conceals violence.

Proverbs 11:3
The integrity of the upright guides them. But the unfaithful are destroyed by their duplicity.

Judy Arnold

Word of the Day - Inner Beauty

In this passage the Bible shows us that beauty is only skin deep as I have heard so many times in my life and it's true. This describes the inner beauty of a woman whose fear of the Lord is to be praised. So many take that as to mean being afraid of God but that not what it means at all. . It is the only appropriate response to our Creator and Redeemer Inner beauty of the heart and soul shines through in everything we do when living for the Lord. And everything we do in our lives we do for God.

To honor him, glorify him and shine his light so others can see what a faithful, awesome God we serve! Remember God sees your spirit man and the beauty within. The prettiest face is nothing if the heart is ugly. In this society we are judged by the way we look, dress and our status financially and for so many people that is their goal. But the old sayings" beauty fades" and" you can't take it with you" are both so true and in the end, what truly matters is your heart for God. Your true heart full of love, compassion, truth, mercy and faithfulness. That beauty shines through to bring lost people to God. That Godly glow, as I describe it is the most beautiful thing and no outer beauty can ever compare to that! Let your heart for God and inner beauty shine and be a blessing to everyone you come in contact with today!! Prayers and Blessings to you all!

Proverbs 27:19 New International Version (NIV)
19 As water reflects the face, so one's life reflects the heart

Proverbs 31:29-31 New International Version (NIV)
29 "Many women do noble things, but you surpass them all." 30 Charm is deceptive, and beauty is fleeting; but a woman who fears the Lord is to be praised. 31 Honor her for all that her hands have done, and let her works bring her praise at the city gate

Word of the Day - Jehovah Jireh

One of the many names of God. Jehovah Jireh our provider! He provides everything we need to live peaceful, holy lives on this earth. Whether we decide to accepted these gifts by surrendering our whole selves to him- body, soul and spirit is our choice. We have two roads put before us-life eternally with the Lord or life in hell for eternity! Seems like a no brainer to me but so many people choose their own way. They turn away from God, from his gospel and salvation. They don't want to be accountable to anyone for their life. That way they do not feel convicted when doing something wrong. God provided a way for us to be back in right relationship with him by sending his only son to die for our sins— now and forever, and give us forgiveness and righteousness in Gods eyes through Jesus. It's so simple yet bears such a great reward for our eternity! Turn to Jehovah Jireh, give him your whole heart and let him show you joy, peace and eternity with him in heaven!

Genesis 22:14 ESV
   So Abraham called the name of that place, "The Lord will provide"; as it is said to this day, "On the mount of the Lord it shall be provided."

Philippians 4:19 ESV
   And my God will supply every need of yours according to his riches in Glory in Christ Jesus.

Judy Arnold

Word of the Day - Jehovah Nissi - Our banner

As the Israelites fought the Amalekites, Moses stood raising the rod of God and prayed in intercession for them. The battle was victorious and Moses built an altar there naming it Jehovah Nissi- my banner. Jehovah—Nissi is our reminder as believers everywhere that we can only be victorious as we honor the name of the Lord, pray to him praise him and believe in him with our whole being

James 5:16
   The prayer of a righteous person is powerful and effective.

Exodus 17:15
   Moses built an altar there and named it Yahweh-Nissi (which means "the LORD is my banner").Word for the Day Jehovah Nissi - our banner

Living God's Word... One Scripture at a Time

Word of the Day - Jehovah Raah- Our Shepherd

This Scripture describe the way a shepherd watches overs his sheep, goes before them, takes care of anything that might harm them. Psalm 23 tells us of all his promises, how he provides for us, refreshes us, restores us, guides us, protects us, shields us from our enemies. Through him we have eternity through salvation! What a powerful promise packed Scripture! There is no situation, problem or anything you have that God doesn't already know about or can't fix. Go to him, trust him and let him be your shepherd, your everything!

Ezekiel 34:11-15
   A shepherd is one who feeds or leads his flock to pasture.

Psalm 80:1
   Oh, give ear, Shepherd of Israel, You who lead Joseph like a flock; you who are enthroned above the cherubim, shine forth

Judy Arnold

Word of the Day - Joy, not happiness

So many people get those two meanings confused. Most of us base our life on how "happy" we are. We look to the world for things or people to make us feel good about ourselves, our lives and the way we live. The world gives us a false sense of what we think is happy but only the Lord can give us real joy! Happiness fades with circumstances but real joy that comes from God stays. Joy is found in God's presence and is everlasting in him. "Our real joy flows in knowing our position in Christ: who we are in him, and what he has done for us. The word joy appears 430 times in the word- happiness only 10 times. Sorrow and suffering will pass, but joy will continues in spite of problems and obstacles. Joy is promised to come and, when it does, it lasts. So let's focus on joy of the Lord that is freely given and last eternally and know Jesus is all we need to be "happy"!!!!

Romans 14:17
  For the kingdom of God is not a matter of eating and drinking but of righteousness and peace and joy in the Holy Spirit.

Romans 15:13
  May the God of hope fill you with all joy and peace in believing, so that by the power of the Holy Spirit you may abound in hope? Rejoice in the Lord always; again I will say, Rejoice.

Living God's Word... One Scripture at a Time

Word of the day:-Just and Judge

Judge-form an opinion or conclusion.

Think about that and think about how many times in our life on a daily basis do we judge other people? So many times we judge people by the way they look, dress, act forming an opinion based on our own filter and beliefs. We couldn't be more wrong for doing such an arrogant thing but we do. We see someone poorly dressed or with tattoos or piercings everywhere and assume they are not appropriate because of the way they look. This is what the word says about that. It's sad to think that we are so quick to judge and tell people their sins instead of looking in our own lives. While we only see the outside, God sees the inside, the heart and only He can judge that. Just -guided by truth, reason, justice, and fairness: We hope to be just in our understanding of such difficult situations.

We serve a just God! "The Rock! His work is perfect, for all His ways are just; A God of faithfulness and without injustice, Righteous and upright is He. He takes care of his children so don't ever try to "get even "with someone. Ask God to intervene Knowing that he has control of every situation, person and situation on the earth. We shouldn't to take things into our own hands when we are hurt offended or done wrong. Instead we should give it to God and let him handle it!

Matthew 7:1-5
 Judging Others
 1 "Do not judge, or you too will be judged. 2For in the same way you judge others, you will be judged, and with the measure you use, it will be measured to you. 3 "Why do you look at the speck of sawdust in your brother's eye and pay no attention to the plank in your own Eye? 4 How can you say to your brother, 'Let me take the speck out of your eye,' when all the time there is a plank in your own eye? 5 You hypocrite, first take the plank out of your

own eye, and then you will see clearly to remove the speck from your brother's eye.

Psalm 9:7-8

But the LORD abides forever; He has established His throne for judgment, and He will judge the world in righteousness; He will execute judgment for the peoples with equity.

Word of the Day - Light of the world and Lord of All!

Jesus, the light of the world. When darkness seems to surround you, let the light of Jesus and his loving arms hold you secure, knowing that he is right there with you- you are never alone. His light and love pierces through the darkness and destroys the storms in your life. As I'm sitting here writing this, the sun is shining through the blinds right in my eyes. I shielded them and realized that the light of Jesus shines bright in each of us.

As we go about our busy day, remember that the Lord of Everything loves you more than you can understand. He is all we should want or ever need and I'm so blessed to let his light shine through me and help lead lost souls to his kingdom! Our bright morning star that Lights up our hearts and our lives so we no longer have to live in darkness! Hallelujah!!

John 8:9-12 New International Version (NIV)
9 At this, those who heard began to go away one at a time, the older ones first, until only Jesus was left, with the woman still standing there. 10 Jesus straightened up and asked her, "Woman, where are they? Has no one condemned you?" 11 "No one, sir," she said. "Then neither do I condemn you," Jesus declared. "Go now and leave your life of sin." Dispute over Jesus' Testimony 12 When Jesus spoke again to the people, he said, ''I am the light of the world. Whoever follows me will never walk in darkness, but will have the light of life."

Philippians 2:9-11 New International Version (NIV)
9 Therefore God exalted him to the highest place and gave him the name that is above every name, 10 that at the name of Jesus every knee should bow, in heaven and on earth and under the earth, 11 and every tongue acknowledge that Jesus Christ is Lord, to the glory of God the Father.

Judy Arnold

Word of the Day—Lost and Found

I once was lost but now I'm found. The most amazing sad and joyful words I ever heard in my life. Being lost in this world today is such an easy thing to do. We get so caught up in all the chaos, being pulled in all directions not knowing which end is up most of the time. It's kind of scary because you are gliding along thinking you are doing good then the devil throws something out of left field and down you go! I didn't live for the Lord a good majority of my life and I certainly paid the consequences of my actions and decisions

I regret that time I was "lost" in the world. It took its toll on me emotionally. Sometimes in our own free will we learn our lessons the hard way but the good thing is, God never stops "wooing" us as I call it. Always trying to bring us back to the path his has for us— a life of peace and joy. As I've always heard, "You can run but you can't hide" and I did for so many years. One day God opened my eyes to his unconditional love for me, showed me who I am to him and I realized how lost I really was. I surrendered my life to him. That was 14 years ago and have never looked back. I love the Lord with everything in me and strive every day to honor him and make him proud

Luke 15:31-32
> "And he said to him, 'Son, you are always with me, and all that is mine is yours. It was fitting to celebrate and be glad, for this your brother was dead, and is alive; he was lost, and is found.'"

Luke 15:10
> Just so, I tell you, there is joy before the angels of God over one sinner who repents.

Word of the Day - Love

Of all the things Jesus instructs us to do in the commandments, I think loving people is the most important one. Love conquers all things and without it we are empty shells. We have to love each other as Jesus loves us, unconditionally. That's real love... This Scripture says it all. I pray each one of you has love in your heart to share it with others and truly show the love of Christ in your lives! Be blessed.

Corinthians 13:4-7

4 Love is patient, love is kind and is not jealous; love does not brag and is not arrogant, 5 does not act unbecomingly; it does not seek its own, is not provoked, does not take into account a wrong suffered, 6 does not rejoice in unrighteousness, but rejoices with the truth; 7 [a]bears all things, believes all things, hopes all things, endures all things.

Psalm 100:1-5

1. Shout for joy to the Lord, all the earth. 2. Worship the Lord with gladness; come before him with joyful songs. 3. Know the Lord is God. It is he who made us, and we are his, we are his people, the sheep of his pasture. 4. Enter the gates with thanksgiving and his courts with praise; give thanks to him and praise his name. 5. For the Lord is good and his love endures forever; his faithfulness continues through all generations.

Judy Arnold

Word of the Day - Make a joyful noise unto the Lord!!!

Praising the Lord in song is one of the most special things I like to do. Everyone worships God in their own way and my favorite is in singing. Although I wouldn't want most people to hear me sing, I love praise and worship at church and singing to the Lord in my car, shower or wherever I feel like I want to. Some people have their closet time, some worship by reading the word. All good things but in my heart I feel like singing to the Lord blesses him but me as well. Giving praise to the Holy one, our healer, our savior, our EVERYTHING makes my heart, soul and mind full of joy and love. So no matter where you are or what you are doing, praise the Lord in your own way and bless his heart with a joyful noise!!!

Psalm 98:4 King James Version (KJV)
4 Make a joyful noise unto the LORD, all the earth: make a loud noise, and rejoice, and sing praise.

Psalm100:1
Make a joyful noise unto the Lord, all ye lands.

Living God's Word... One Scripture at a Time

Word of the Day - Malice

What is the definition of Malice? ...desire to inflict injury, harm, or suffering on another, either because of a hostile impulse or out of deep-seated meanness. That is something I pray no one will ever have against me. Wanting to hurt someone or "get" back at them is such an ungodly thing to do! I realize sometimes people do things to hurt or make us angry but taking revenge or making them "pay" is not our job. God sees all things and is righteous and just and will take care of things in his way and time. He definitely doesn't need our help nor does he want us to. The battle is mine says the Lord! He sees the evil in this world and he takes care of his children. Nobody or nothing is worth the risk of hurting your right standing with God. He is always working in your behalf to remedy bad situations and taking care of it ourselves hinders his plan. Let God "fix" the problems and people in your life that bring you to the point of anger or malice. Don't let those people or situations cause you to Sin- that's exactly what Satan is striving for!!!

Ephesians 4:31-32 ESV
> Let all bitterness and wrath and anger and clamor and slander be put away from you, along with all malice. Be kind to one another, tenderhearted, forgiving one another, as God in Christ forgave you.

James 1:19-20 ESV
> Know this, my beloved brothers: let every person be quick to hear, slow to speak, slow to anger; for the anger of man does not produce the righteousness of God.

Judy Arnold

Word of the Day - Mercy

I strive so hard daily to be a loving, kind, compassionate person. To do what is right in God's eyes but being a sinner, I Mess up daily. This race we are running is hard and there will be "bumps" in the road that throw us off the path. God understands that but that's what's so great about mercy and forgiveness? His mercies are new every morning. We have to repent, pull ourselves up, dust ourselves off and steadily push forward. The end goal, eternity with our savior is worth anything and everything we endure in this life on earth. This is not our home and one day soon we will be in glory praising Jesus and the pain and hardships of this race won't even be a memory. Keep your eyes on God!! Fight the good fight and pursue Gods heart! Love and hugs to you all in the Lord!

Romans 2:26
> God "will repay each person according to what they have done." But go and learn what this means: 'I desire mercy, not sacrifice.' For I have not come to call the righteous, but sinners.

Matthew 2:13
> "The Lord bless you and keep you; the Lord make his face shine on you and be gracious to you; the Lord turn his face toward you and give you peace."

Word of the Day - Mighty

Who is the Lord Our God? The most holy one, mighty in power, mighty in strength, mighty in wisdom, mighty in glory! Our savior, our king! He goes before us and fights our battles! He has our back in every situation. It's hard for me to comprehend that the One that made the universe that put the stars in the skies, that moves mountains in our way loves me!! An all-powerful loving God cares about my life, my happiness so much that he catches every tear I cry. Can you just imagine that? I can't, not really but the battles and storms I've experienced in my life that seemed impossible melted away when my God stepped in and I had the victory. As I walk my daily journey on this earth, no matter what comes my way, I know God will be right there with me every step of the way and that's my anchor I hold on to.

Luke 1:49
   For the Mighty One has done great things for me; and holy is His name.

Psalm 147:5
   Great is our Lord and abundant in strength; His understanding is infinite

Judy Arnold

Word of the Day - Miracles

Do you believe in miracles? When I read so many Scriptures about all the miracles Jesus did in his short life on earth, I am just amazed. Yet the people still doubted he was the Messiah. Can you imagine after all the wonders they saw yet still didn't believe? So in our time we have the word to read about these things but do we really believe miracles can happen?

Well I can tell you with no doubt in my mind that I'm absolutely positive they do! My husband was on his death bed at age 52, in a coma and about to be put on dialysis for fungal meningitis. The Dr. told me to call my kids and family for he wouldn't probably make it through the day. As I sat in ICU staring at him dying thinking this can't be real, my faith rose up in me and I spoke out loud to God - we need a miracle! I put him in God's hands praying his will. He woke up three days later and his first words were, "for the love of God!" He improved daily and 32 days later we went home - he was totally healed! The Doctors called it a miracle, what else could they say!

I was healed later in the year from hep-c, a torn rotator cuff that needed surgery and many other things. So don't ever think your problem is too big for our God!

Pray, believe, wait on God!!! He is a miracle working Savior!!!

Jeremiah 32:27
  27 "I am the LORD, the God of all mankind. Is anything too hard for me?

Job 52:8-9
  8 But if I were you, I would appeal to God; I would lay my cause before him. 9 He performs wonders that cannot be fathomed, miracles that cannot be counted.

Living God's Word... One Scripture at a Time

Words of the Day - My Rock, My Refuge, My Shield

What a mighty God we serve! The Lord is my rock in which I stand firm and will not be shaken! The Lord is my refugee where I run to in times of trouble. He hides me in the shadow of his wings, safe and sound from the attacks of ungodly people that try to snare me. The Lord is my shield that covers me and secures me from the fiery darts of Satan. With him I have safety, security, protection, forgiveness and most of all love. Without him I am fearful, sinful with no hope like sinking sand. He deserves all our praise and honor for without him we are nothing. As I think on these things, my mind is at peace and my heart is joyful for I know I have eternity with the Lord forever!!! Be blessed in everything you put your hands to today in the mighty name of Jesus!!

2 Samuel 22:1-4 English Standard Version (ESV)
David's Song of Deliverance
22 And David spoke to the Lord the words of this song on the day when the Lord delivered him from the hand of all his enemies, and from the hand of Saul. 2 He said, The Lord is my rock and my fortress and my deliverer, 3 my God, my rock, in whom I take refuge, my shield, and the horn of my salvation, my stronghold and my refuge, my savior; you save me from violence. 4 I call upon the Lord, who is worthy to be praised, and I am saved from my enemies.

2 Samuel 22:31-33 English Standard Version (ESV)
31 This God—his way is perfect; the word of the Lord proves true; he is a shield for all those who take refuge in him. 32 "For who is God, but the Lord? And who is a rock, except our God? 33 This God is my strong refuge and has made my way blameless.

Judy Arnold

Word of the Day - Nature

As we go about our busy days and lives do us really see this beautiful earth God has so graciously given us to live in? Most of us take the trees, the grass, and the beautiful blue skies and even a cool breeze for granted. We are so distracted by social media, cell phone, I Pads, computers, watching TV that we miss the best free gifts God has blessed us with.

Do you ever stop to pick a wild flower and smell it? Or watch the wind bending a tree from side to side? Or listen to the birds sing or the squirrels chattering in the trees? When you go to the beach, do you sit and listen to the waves or watch the sea gulls flying overhead? Do you ever take time to take your shoes off and walk barefoot in the grass, feeling the soft coolness beneath your feet? Do you sit outside at night and watch the stars twinkle? God made all these perfect awesome things for us to enjoy yet we're too caught up in life to enjoy freely given nature. Simple things that can give us peace and truly bless our lives. I look around and I see nature, its beauty and gracefulness and I'm in awe of God. I can only just imagine what heaven looks like- can you?? Stop and take a moment every day to enjoy the blessings God has given to us, appreciate it and thank him for loving us so very much to give us such beauty on this earth!

Psalm 19:1
God's Glory in Nature
The heavens are telling of the glory of God; and their expanse is declaring the work of His hands

John 1:3
3 Through him all things were made; without him nothing was made that has been made.

Living God's Word... One Scripture at a Time

Word of the Day - Omnipotent and Messiah.

Om-nip-o-tent adjective

1 (of a deity) having unlimited power; able to do anything.

Synonyms: a powerful, almighty, supreme, preeminent, most high; noun. God

Messiah the Hebrew word "Mashiach" which means "Anointed One." What a mighty, powerful God we serve! Able to move mountains in our way, yet catch every tear, able to calm the raging sea yet hold us safe in the shadow of his wings, able to create a universe by just speaking it into existence, yet gentle enough to heal a broken heart. This God that loves us unconditionally, that sent his son to die for a sinner like me, wants a relationship with us, his children. He sent us Jesus, the Messiah, the anointed one. The one without sin to make a way for us to be righteous or in right standing with the Father. Baby Jesus, lying in a manager so innocent sent to die for us! What love, what compassion he has for us! I'm humbled that he did that for me and I will praise Him, worship him and honor my Jesus, my Savior, my Redeemer, and my Lord!! Not just at Christmas but every day of my life and forever in heaven. I can only imagine how I will feel when I bow before the king of kings and see my Jesus face to face!!! What an awesome, glorious day that will be!!

Exodus 15:6
  6. "Thy right hand, O LORD, is majestic in power, Thy right hand, 0 LORD, shatters the enemy"

Isaiah 45:12
  "It is I who made the earth, and created man upon it. I stretched out the heavens with my hands, and I ordained all their host"

Judy Arnold

Word of the Day - Omniscient and Omnipresent

Omniscient-All knowing, all wise, all seeing. You ever think about God like the above description? I think if we stopped long enough to really understand this we would have far less chaos and problems in our lives. All knowing—he knows everything about us, our faults and failures, our dreams and wishes, our very thoughts. Yet we fret and worrying about everything and every situation that Satan throws at us. He sees everything and in his perfect wisdom, knows what we need. No situation or problem surprises God because he knows our future. He directs our paths and even when we stray and fall, He is there picking us up, dusting us off and putting us back on the path he has for our lives. So don't worry about tomorrow for God is already there, He knows, He sees and He goes before us to make a way! Omnipresent-present everywhere. No matter where you are, what you are going through, God is there. He walks besides us through our weakest moments and our most joyous times. .He is there in our sickness, through the most trying times, through the fiercest storm, the loss of a loved one, through job loss and all hardships. He is with us and never leaves us. He is our very present help in time of need!

Jeremiah 29:11
> For I know the plans I have for you," declares the LORD, "plans to prosper you and not to harm you, plans to give you hope and a future.

Psalm 139:4
> "Before a word is on my tongue you know it completely, O Lord"

Word of the Day - One

There is only one God, maker of the universe, the Holy One. He is out Lord and Savior to who deserves all glory and praise. Look to the one who is our everything, the one and only true living God!

Psalm 139:4
  Before word is on my tongue you, Lord, Know it completely.

Ephesians 4:4-8
  4 There is one body and one Spirit, just as you were called to one hope when you were called; 5 one Lord, one faith, one baptism; 6 one God and Father of all, who is over all and through all and in all. 7 But to each one of us grace has been given as Christ apportioned it. 8 This is why it says: When he ascended on high, he took many captives and gave gifts to his people.

Judy Arnold

Word of the Day -Peace through Faith

Peace with God through Jesus. What an amazing statement. This entire Scripture shows us that through him we can endure anything, fear nothing and trust a loving God that has our best interests at heart. Everything we go through makes us stronger so we can endure the hardest things, hope for a good out come and have peace. Knowing that God has it. Nothing surprises him and he is on the throne working things out for us before we even ask. Not like the world gives but only through Jesus and having the Faith to trust him with our lives, children and family. That's real peace, real faith and something we ALL need in our everyday |lives... trust our loving Father in EVERYTHING!! He will see you through if you just have faith! We are truly blessed!!!

Colossians 3:15
   Let the peace of Christ rule in your hearts, since as members of one body you were called to peace. And be thankful.

Psalm 85:8
   I will listen to what God the Lord says; he promises peace to his people, his faithful servants-but let them not turn to folly.

Living God's Word... One Scripture at a Time

Word of the Day - Perfect Love and Mercy

All these things describe the one who IS perfect love... Jesus! Love everyone like Jesus, unconditionally with a forgiving heart! God loved us so much that he sacrificed his son just so we could be in right relationship with him again and Jesus gave his life so we could be Righteous in our Fathers eyes... that's real love! We serve a faithful, merciful and loving God that cherishes us more than we can comprehend. As we celebrate the birth of Jesus on Christmas day remember... that precious baby grew up to be a man. Human, suffering a horrific death on the cross to give us eternity in heaven!!! Thank him and praise him with your whole heart and soul! Sing Glory to our King!!!

Hebrews 4:16
> 16 Let us then approach God's throne of grace with confidence, so that we may receive mercy and find grace to help us in our time of need.

Ephesians 2:4-5
> But God, being rich in mercy, because of the great love with which he loved us, even when we were dead in our trespasses, made us alive together with Christ by grace you have been saved.

Judy Arnold

Word of the Day - Perfect Peace

I absolutely love this Scripture! You keep him in perfect peace whose mind is stayed on you, because he trusts in you. Wow, perfect peace as only the Lord can give us. There is anything but peace in this chaotic world for those living for themselves and not for God. We all have our troubles and trials in this life but knowing the Lord, having faith and trusting him with every aspect of your life brings perfect peace.

Philippians 4:6-7
"Be anxious for nothing, but in everything by prayer and supplication, with thanksgiving, let Your requests be made known to God; and the peace of God, which surpasses all understanding, will guard your hearts and minds through Christ Jesus."

Isaiah 26:1-4 English Standard Version (ESV)
You Keep Him in Perfect Peace
1 In that day this song will be sung in the land of Judah: "We have a strong city; he sets up salvation as walls and bulwarks. 2 Open the gates that the righteous nation that keeps faith may enter in. 3 you keep him in perfect peace whose mind is stayed on you, because he trusts in you. 4 Trust in the Lord forever, for the Lord God is an everlasting rock.

Word of the Day - Prince of Peace and Prophet

Our Prince of Peace- JESUS!! Our Wonderful counselor, Lord of Life, Lord of all...EMMANUEL! A child born in a manger surrounded by filth that came to cleanse the world! This innocent baby that would one day save us from our sins, give us hope and eternity in heaven forever! Prophet- a person regarded as an inspired teacher or proclaimer of the will of God. As Jesus walked among his own people teaching them about the Kingdom of God, they doubted and even mocked him. A carpenter's son they watched grow from a baby was proclaiming to be Gods son. He did so many miracles and yet they didn't believe him. If they had only realized they were in the presence of God himself, how blessed and humbled they would have been! They got to witness the work of his hand yet didn't believe. Sometimes seeing is not believing but trusting in Jesus, our one true savior is our truth and way to eternity with the Father! I love seeing miracles happen but I don't need them to know who holds my life in his hands and I'm blessed beyond belief to know him, to serve him and one day spend eternity in heaven with him!

Isaiah 9:6
"For a child will be born to us, a son will be given to us; And the government will rest on His shoulders; And His name will be called Wonderful Counselor, Mighty God, Eternal Father, Prince of Peace"

John 14:27 New International Version (NIV)
27 Peace I leave with you; my peace I give you. I do not give to you as the world gives. Do not let your hearts be troubled and do not be afraid.

Judy Arnold

Word of the Day- Promises

This Scripture reveals to us just how very blessed and favored of the Lord we are! Not only did he make salvation so simply by just believing in him and who he is but he gave us instructions for everything we need to live a Holy life!

Living our lives with these qualities not only enriches our own lives but through them shows the light of Jesus within us to everyone we meet. That opens the door to witness to them about Jesus and what a difference living for him will make in their life! What an awesome opportunity that is! But also these things make us who we are in Christ- his nature, his love, his goodness and that is what being a child of God is all about- being His! As today as you read the Scripture remember that God didn't just give us the 10 commandments and said... Here- do this but gave us his promises to show us how!! That's our good good Father! Have a blessed day!

2 Peter 1:3-8 New International Version (NIV)
Confirming One's Calling and Election
3 His divine power has given us everything we need for a godly life through our knowledge of him who called us by his own glory and goodness. 4 Through these he has given us his very great and precious promises, so that through them you may participate in the divine nature, having escaped the corruption in the world caused by evil desires. 5 For this very reason, make every effort to add to your faith goodness; and to goodness, knowledge; 6 and to knowledge, self-control; and to self-control, perseverance; and to perseverance, godliness; 7 and to godliness, mutual affection; and to mutual affection, love. 8 For if you possess these qualities in increasing measure, they will keep you from being ineffective and unproductive in your knowledge of our Lord Jesus Christ

Exodus 14:14
The Lord will fight for you; you need only to be still.

Word of the Day - Prosperity

The dictionary describes it as the state of being prosperous. "As humans we tend to classify it as being wealthy, money wise, but being prosperous in God's word is so much more. He provides much more meaningful ways of prosperity that we sometimes don't realize. Ease, comfort, security and wellbeing. God's promises to sustain us, to give us life more abundantly with these things and so much more. We are secure in him, through our struggles, in our storms and in our eternal salvation. I don't know about you but having the knowledge and promise from our loving God means so much more than money could ever buy. We prosper because of his love, mercy, forgiveness and his promise of eternity in heaven with him. I don't think I could ever ask or want anything more. No worries my friends in Christ- God has it taken care of!!

Jeremiah 17:10
  I the Lord search the heart and test the mind, to give every man according to his ways, according to the fruit of his deeds.

Proverbs 6:2
  Commit to the Lord whatever you do, and he will establish your plans

Judy Arnold

Word of the Day-Purpose of Grace

Grace- unmerited favor- in other words favor we don't deserve. But grace is freely given and as this Scripture reveals was given to us in Jesus before the beginning of time! Wow. Let that sink in a minute. I am still in awe how much God loves a sinner like me. That he gave his sons life for me and through Jesus, we have favor we otherwise wouldn't have or surely deserve. Grace to make it through the roughest times, grace when a situation seems impossible, and grace in our sin when we least deserve it. I can't imagine surviving my life without it nor do I ever want to find out. We have a Mighty God that goes before us and makes a way through his grace, his unending love and compassion for his children. I know I'm truly blessed and highly favored of the Lord and by his grace I am saved because of Jesus and his sacrifice. I'm thankful for that every single day! May the joy of the Lord fill your heart and soul today!

One of my favorite Scriptures on grace...

Ephesians 2:8-9 New International Version (NIV)
 8 For it is by grace you have been saved, through faith—and this is not from yourselves, it is the gift of God— 9 not by works, so that no one can boast.

2 Timothy 1:9-10 New International Version (NIV)
 9 He has saved us and called us to a holy life—not because of anything we have done but because of his own purpose and grace. This grace was given us in Christ Jesus before the beginning of time, 10 but it has now been revealed through the appearing of our Savior, Christ Jesus, who has destroyed death and has brought life and immortality to light through the gospel

Living God's Word... One Scripture at a Time

Word of the Day - Putting God first

What bondage, what addiction, what sickness, and what impossible situation has God brought YOU out of? Do you put God first in every aspect of your life trusting him in all things? God brought us from sinners to righteous, from bondage to freedom, from lost to found, from unworthy to redeem!! He gave his only son to die for us—to be in right relationship with him again. We are so "busy" in our lives with errands, children, work, friends and just enjoying our life that we don't have "time for God". Why is that? We make time for everything we consider important forgetting the one who made our salvation possible. The one that saved us from eternity in hell and gave us everlasting life! God should be the first thought on your mind when we wake up and the last thought when we close our eyes. Constantly thanking him and praising him for the ultimate gift he gave us. He should be the most important thing in our lives. We have so many "idles" that keep us distracted from serving God as we should. Anything we deem more important than God is an idle and as his word says-he is a jealous God. He deserves all the honor, glory and praise for everything in our lives. Remember to put the Lord first and foremost in your life. Love on him and thank him for the many blessings and miracles in your life!

Jeremiah 29:11 (NIV)
  For I know the plans I have for you, plans to prosper you and not to harm you, plans to give you hope and a future.

Exodus 20:1-6 English Standard Version (ESV)
  The Ten Commandments
20 And God spoke all these words, saying, 2 "I am the LORD your God, who brought you out of the land of Egypt, out of the house of slavery. 3"You shall have no other gods before me. 4"You shall not make for yourself a carved image, or any likeness of anything that is in heaven above, or that is in the earth beneath, or that is in the water under the earth. 5 You shall not bow down to them or serve them, for I the LORD your God am a

jealous God, visiting the iniquity of the fathers on the children to the third and the fourth generation of those who hate me, 6 but showing steadfast love to thousands of those who love me and keep my commandments.

Word of the Day - Rebellion

When a person "rebels," it simply means that they refuse to come under the authority of someone who is above them. God HATES rebellion, and says it "is as the sin of witchcraft. The Bible also says this about rebellion: Rebellion grieves the Holy Spirit and causes Him to be their enemy and fight against them. Many people rebelled in the Bible, and paid a great price for doing so. Moses rebelled and was not allowed to enter the Promised Land. There are so many other examples of rebellion or disobedience to God and the consequences. So many times we choose to do our" own thing" and ignore what God says about situations and how to handle them. We ultimately face the consequences of our actions. So when in doubt, always go to Gods word, be obedient to his commands, listen to him and trust him- in all things! Remember to have a blessed day and do something nice for someone today— you might just be the one who gets blessed!!

Joshua 1:18
"Anyone who rebels against your command and does not obey your words in all that you command him, shall be put to death; only be strong and courageous."

1 Samuel 15:23
For rebellion is like the sin of divination, and arrogance like the evil of idolatry. Because you have rejected the word of the LORD, he has rejected

Judy Arnold

Word of the Day - Redeemed!!

Every time I hear the word redeemed it brings to mind the song Redeemed by Big Daddy Weave. It's my mine and my husband's favorite song and it touches my heart for a couple reasons. My hubby is a precious man of God, very strong and quite but to see him brought to tears by the word redeemed makes me realize how important that word really is. Redeemed: gain or regain possession of (something) in exchange for payment. Think about that definition: Our salvation- Jesus paid the ultimate price, death on the cross in exchange for our eternity in heaven! Kind of makes the word have more of a significant importance when you realize what he did for all of us. How great a love is it for God to sacrifice his son, to die that horrible death on the cross and for Jesus, our Lord and Savior to go through that for sinners like us! That is unconditional love, death for redemption!

Ephesians 1:7
   In Him we have redemption through His blood, the forgiveness of our trespasses, according to the riches of His grace

1 Corinthians 1:30
   But by His doing you are in Christ Jesus, who became to us wisdom from God, and righteousness and sanctification, and redemption,

Living God's Word... One Scripture at a Time

Word of the Day - Refuge and Blessings

Sometimes we get so busy and caught up in everyday life we miss the smallest blessings. Things other people call luck or coincidence when blessings come their way. If we would just slow down and "smell the roses "as we have always heard, we would see the hand of God in the simplest things. Everybody notices big blessings but the small ones evade us because we're not focused on God. Every lost you cell phone or misplaced your keys? How many of you get frantic and search everywhere instead of asking God to help? You would be surprised how quick he answers because he wants to bless us. Every been in a hurry and ran to Walmart only to find the parking lot full but turn the corner and there is a parking space right in front by the door? That's a blessing but how many of us stop and thank God for that? I've had people say well that's just luck and in a way I guess that's true. I'm "lucky" that I have a Father that loves me so much that he would do such a simple thing to help me.

We need to pay less attention to this chaotic world and more to the everyday blessings we miss...isn't it a blessing to have a God we can run to, confide in, pour our heart out to, trusting him with every aspect of our life? Our refuge not just in times of trouble but in every instance of our lives. It's my peace and comfort knowing the Lord is my refuge, my strength, my blessing and all I will ever need or want in this world. Eternity with our Father in heaven is a blessing I cherish and look forward to when my race here on earth is finished!!!

Genesis 17:1-2 English Standard Version (ESV)
Abraham and the Covenant of Circumcision: 17 When Abram was ninety-nine years old the Lord appeared to Abram and said to him, ''I am God Almighty; walk before me, and be blameless, 2 that I may make my covenant between me and you, and may multiply you greatly."

Genesis 49:22-26 English Standard Version (ESV)

22 Joseph is a fruitful bough, a fruitful bough by a spring; his branches run over the wall. 23 The archers bitterly attacked him, shot at him, and harassed him severely, 24 yet his bow remained unmoved; his arms were made agile by the hands of the Mighty One of Jacob (from there is the Shepherd, the Stone of Israel), 25 by the God of your father who will help you, by the Almighty who will bless you with blessings of heaven above, blessings of the deep that crouches beneath, blessings of the breasts and of the womb. 26 The blessings of your father are mighty beyond the blessings of my parents, up to the bounties of the everlasting hills. May they be on the head of Joseph, and on the brow of him who was set apart from his brothers.

Word of the Day - Refuge

Jesus, our place of refuge from the storms in our life. Our very present help in time of need. I have heard that so many times in my life at church and in Bible studies but do we really understand what that means? Since I have been saved I have looked back on my former life, all the mistakes I made and just how very lost I was. But yet I can see so many instances where God intervened, stopping me from pain and suffering of my own doing. Even when I was yet a sinner he was watching out for me. Stubborn as I was and as much as I ran from him in the opposite direction, He never left me.

Of all the wondrous miracles he has done since I surrendered to him, and there have been many, those unsaved "lost" times he protected me, mean just as much as the saved ones. Just knowing he loved me that much and never gave up on me brings tears to my eyes and a smile. Yes, Jesus is my refuge, my savior, my shelter in the storm, my hope and my everything!!!

Psalm 46:1
  God is our refuge and strength, a very present help in trouble.

Psalm 91:2
  I will say to the LORD, "My refuge and my fortress, My God, in whom I trust!"

Judy Arnold

Word of the Day - Rejoice!!

No matter what your circumstance or what storm you may be going through today, rejoice in the Lord!! He gives us strength to go through things we never could on our own. He walks through the fire with us, protecting us from harm. Our joy doesn't come from things, people or circumstances. Those things may make you happy and are temporary but the Joy that comes from the Lord never fades. As followers of Christ, we should rejoice always, in good times and bad but sometimes that isn't easy to do.

We rejoice because of what God has done through our Lord Jesus Christ and Salvation- to spend eternity in heaven. Be joyful always, pray at all times, and be thankful in all circumstances.

Psalm 106:1 (BRG)
> Praise you the Lord. 0 give thanks unto the Lord; for he is good: for his mercy endureth for ever Prayers and blessings to all of you today

Living God's Word... One Scripture at a Time

Word of the Day - "Remember"

How often we forget the many promises the Lord has given us in His Holy Word. We go about our busy lives worrying about a multitude of problems, forgetting who God really is. Remember that he tells us that He will NEVER leave us or forsake us! Remember that when you are walking through a storm that he is right there with you every step of the way! Remember that God is not a man and does not lie. Whatever he promises you, He will do it. In HIS time, in HIS way and for HIS purpose for our lives! But last and most important, Remember He is God, the maker of all things. The Great I AM! Nothing can stand against him. He is truth, wisdom, peace, comfort, healing and the true meaning of unconditional love! In him, we are truly free!!! Have a awesome blessed day and may God bless everything you put your hands to today!! Hugs!

Habakkuk 3:17-19 English Standard Version (ESV)
 Habakkuk Rejoices in the Lord
 17 Though the fig tree should not blossom, nor fruit be on the vines, the produce of the olive fail and the fields yield no food, the flock be cut off from the fold and there be no herd in the stalls, 18 yet I will rejoice in the Lord; I will take joy in the God of my salvation. 19 God, the Lord, is my strength; he makes my feet like the deer's; he makes me tread on my high places.

Isaiah 46:8-11 New King James Version (NKJV)
 "Remember this, and show yourselves men; recall to mind, O you transgressors. 9 Remember the former things of old, for I am God, and there is no other; I am God, and there is none like me, 10 Declaring the end from the beginning, and from ancient times things that are not yet done, saying, 'My counsel shall stand, and I will do all my pleasure,' 11 Calling a bird of prey from the east, the man who executes my counsel, from a far country. Indeed I have spoken it; I will also bring it to pass. I have purposed it; I will also do it.

Judy Arnold

Word of the Day - Respect

People are God's creation and no matter what we think of them, God created each one of us for a purpose and each one of us are different. That's a good thing - can you imagine if we were all alike? How boring an existence that would be! No matter what your purpose is or the next person, we should all respect each other and what they do. Treat people with respect as you would want to be treated for it is Gods will for us to do so. We should love our family of believers, show them respect, honor and love as the Lord so lavishes on us! Children should obey their parents out of love and respect. As we treat each other as the word says, this world will be a better place for them.

1 Peter 2:17
   17 Show proper respect to everyone, love the family of believers, fear God, and honor the emperor.

1 Thessalonians 5:12-13 ESV
   We ask you, brothers, to respect those who labor among you and are over you in the Lord and admonish you, and to esteem them very highly in love because of their work. Be at peace among yourselves.

Living God's Word... One Scripture at a Time

Word of the Day - Restoration

This world and its craziness seems to want to break us down and stop us from the joy and peace the Lord wants for us. Satan comes to steal, kill and destroy but the Lord comes to restore! I absolutely love that Scripture! We get so caught up in everyday life, we lose the joy we felt when we first got saved. That feeling of peace and overwhelming joy of wanting to be in God's presence all the time. Sometimes that gets lost in the chaos and we need a refreshing, Restoring and renewing of our mind and spirit.

A clean heart free from sin, a loyal spirit to the one true God, obedience to our father and the joy of our salvation. God wants us to be restored, healthy and whole, Full of joy and peace, and to be free! Let God restore your heart and give you peace no matter what storm you might be going through. He is the giver of life, the Holy one and our risen Savior! Give your heart and soul to him and see the change in you through surrender. Peace beyond understanding and joy everlasting.

Psalm 23:13 English Standard Version
  He restores my soul. He leads me in paths of righteousness for his name's sake.

Isaiah 41:13
  For I am the LORD your God who takes hold of your right hand and says to you, do not fear; I will help you.

Judy Arnold

Word of the Day - Righteous Living

Isn't it awesome that, as born again believers, we are righteous in Gods eyes? Not by our own doing but through the righteousness of Our Lord Jesus Christ! When God looks at us he sees us as righteous, holy, looking at our born again inner man, our spirit. He doesn't see our sin because of the sacrifice and unconditional love Jesus showed for us by dying on the cross. In thankfulness, gratitude and love for him we should in return live a righteous life without sin. Our very witness in everyday life should show the love and light of Jesus.

Showing faithfulness, honor, truthfulness, compassion, mercy and love to everyone that crosses our path, living righteous in every aspect of our life. Not just because we have to but because we want to. We can never in ourselves do enough, give enough or pray enough to be righteous. But praise to Jesus our Lord and Savior and his righteousness, we are again in right standing with the Father. Not one of us are righteous in our own selves but our righteousness is based on what Jesus did on the cross. We are now righteous in Gods eyes because Jesus became our sin and his sacrifice on the cross put us again in right standing with God. Through this righteousness we find peace and confidence. I'm in awe that Jesus would give his life for a sinner like me but I'm thankful that he loved me so much and that through his shed blood I am free. As a result, will spend eternity in the presence of the holy, pure, loving, kind, gentle, and righteous God. When you are tempted to sin remember the pain and sacrifice our loving Savior went through for us so that forever we would be righteous in the eyes of our loving Father in heaven.

Proverbs 12:1-3 New International Version (NIV)
12 Whoever loves discipline loves knowledge, but whoever hates correction is stupid. 2 Good people obtain favor from the Lord, but he condemns those who devise wicked schemes. 3 No one

can be established through wickedness, but the righteous cannot be uprooted.

Proverbs 12:19-20 New International Version (NIV)
19 Truthful lips endure forever, but a lying tongue lasts only a moment. 20 Deceit is in the hearts of those who plot evil, but those who promote peace have joy2 Corinthians 5:21 He made Him who knew no sin to be sin on our behalf, so that we might become the righteousness of God in Him.

Judy Arnold

Word of the Day - Risen Lord and My Rock

Jesus!!! Our Risen Lord! King of Kings and Lord of Lords, Savior, Redeemer, Our Rock and Solid Foundation. On Christ the solid rock I stand, all other ground is sinking sand! I love that old hymn and the words ring true. As God as our strong foundation, nothing can come against us and stand! We are safe in the arms of our Savior that conquered death and the grave and rose again! He is Risen, He is our Rock, and He is all we will ever need! JESUS! Praise the Risen King, fall down before him and worship him!

1 Peter 1:3
Let us give thanks to the God and Father of our Lord Jesus Christ! Because of his great mercy he gave us new life by raising Jesus Christ from death. This fills us with a living hope.

Matthew 7:24-26 New International Version (NIV)
The Wise and Foolish Builders
24 "Therefore everyone who hears these words of mine and puts them into practice is like a wise man who built his house on the rock. 25 The rain came down, the streams rose, and the winds blew and beat against that house; yet it did not fall, because it had its foundation on the rock. 26 but everyone who hears these words of mine and does not put them into practice is like a foolish man who built his house on sand.

Word of the Day – Sanctification

We have so many problems these days. Our many health issues, chaos in our emotions, bitterness from hurt than can literally destroy not only our lives but our relationship with God as well. The Lord has a solution in his word for each of these things and so much more. Satan loves to intrude into our lives in any way possible keeping us distracted and our eyes off God... and he's pretty darn good at it.

We live in a fallen, evil world where disease is destroying our bodies- but God has healing in his hands for us. Satan tries to destroy our emotions by causing chaos and hurtful things- but God has peace for us. Satan manipulates us in situations in ways to make us sin, thinking we will lose favor in Gods eyes- but God has sanctification- setting His children apart at salvation.

We are holy and righteous in his eyes. His word shows us that he has made a way for us in every situation. By keeping our eyes on him and not this world, living his word, believing in Jesus and being faithful, we can have healing, peace and sanctification but more than that we are assured eternal life. What a loving God we serve!! Hug someone today and tell them there is hope in Jesus

Romans 8:2-11
> However, you are not in the flesh but in the Spirit, if indeed the Spirit of God dwells in you but if anyone does not have the Spirit of Christ, he does not belong to Him. If Christ is in you, though the body is dead because of sin, yet the spirit is alive because of righteousness. But if the Spirit of Him who raised Jesus from the dead dwells in you, He who raised Christ Jesus from the dead will also give life to your mortal bodies through His Spirit who dwells in you.

Ephesians 1:13

And you also were included in Christ when you heard the message of truth, the gospel of your salvation. When you believed, you were marked in him with a seal, the promised Holy Spirit

Word of the Day - Savior and Son of Man

Savior-Jesus Christ- redeemer of sin and saver of souls. What a sacrifice, what a savior, what mercy, grace and forgiveness given freely to a sinner like me. I'll never understand that kind of unconditional love Jesus has for us but I am so humbled and grateful. My life saved by his death and my eternity sealed by his resurrection and ascension into heaven. Born into this world an innocent child to experience everything we do, to understand our trials and tribulations and eventually die a horrible painful death for our sins.

An act of love we can never repay but we can live for him, love him, honor and praise him and share that love with everyone we can. As this year comes to an end and a new one is about to begin remember the love God has for us, the promise of a future forever with him in heaven!!!

Son of Man - Jesus was fully God (John 1:1), but He was also a human being (John 1:14)

Judy Arnold

Word of the Day - Saved

What does the word say about being saved? The most joyful thing that can ever happen to you. Confessing with your mouth that you are a sinner in need of a savior, lost. That Jesus is the Son of God that he died on the cross for your sins and rose from the dead ascended into heaven and sits at the right hand of the Father interceding for us. Surrendering your heart and body and soul to our Savior and living our lives according to word.

We are free from sin, past, present and future, forgiven, justified in Gods eyes through the righteousness of Jesus. Free to receive eternal life through the sacrifice of Jesus on the cross. To experience new birth in your spirit man and have a personal relationship with the savior! We have hope because he lives and face tomorrow knowing we are promised eternity in heaven. What a sacrifice, what a miracle for us and what a savior!!' Give your life to Jesus. It will be the best decision you ever make in your life!!!

Acts 4:12
    And there is salvation in no one else; for there is no other name under heaven that has been given among men by which we must be saved.

Romans 10:9 ESV
    Because, if you confess with your mouth that Jesus is Lord and believe in your heart that God raised him from the dead, you will be saved.

Living God's Word... One Scripture at a Time

Word of the Day - Self Absorbed Self-centered

All about me is what a majority of this generation is made of and it's really horrifying! I see it everywhere, people running people off the road in such a hurry to get somewhere. Or people weaving all over the road while texting oblivious of the accidents they could cause. I see so many of the younger generation disrespectful to their parents when they don't buy them things they want. Not realizing they worked their whole lives to get what they have. Couples who have children then expect their parents to keep them while they party, have fun and live their lives with no responsibility.

All these Scripture warn about doing evil, putting yourselves before others and God, the worst thing you can do. We need to wake up, start putting others needs before ourselves and put pride aside. I love the quote Joyce Meyer makes when she walks across the stage like a robot saying" what about me but what about me?" This "Me" generation needs to get back to basics. Read the word and put GOD first in our lives, get out of our selfish ways and love God then we will have blessed lives!

Philippians 2:3-4 ESV
> Do nothing from rivalry or conceit, but in humility count others more significant than yourselves. Let each of you look not only to his own interests, but also to the interests of others.

Romans 12:3 ESV
> For by the grace given to me I say to everyone among you not to think of himself more highly than he ought to think, but to think with sober judgment, each according to the measure of faith that God has assigned

Judy Arnold

Word of the Day - Sing!!

Can you imagine being Moses and getting to see God do such a breath taking miraculous thing? Well I would have been in awe of the mighty power of our Father... how many times has God swallowed up your "enemy" in a hopeless situation? Financial problems, sickness, emotional situations where it felt giant in size with no possible solution but God stepped in and made impossible things possible... nothing is too hard for God!! Did you praise him and thank him for making a way when there wasn't one?

That's our God - mighty in power, able to do more than we can imagine. I sing to the Lord all the time, although he's probably holding his hands over his ears the whole time lol. The word says make a joyful noise to the Lord. So many times I don't have time to sit down to read the word but as I'm driving I Sing and praise God through the words of the songs on the radio. It's my way of praising God. He deserves so much more than I could ever do or say. Today sing songs of praise and thanksgiving to our mighty God for all he has done for you!

Psalm 59:16
> But as for me, I shall sing of your strength; Yes, I shall joyfully sing of your lovingkindness in the morning, for you have been my stronghold and a refuge in the day of my distress

Psalm 59:17
> O my strength, I will sing praises to you; For God is my stronghold, the God who shows me lovingkindness.

Living God's Word... One Scripture at a Time

Word of the Day - Storms in our lives

What are the storms in your life? The ones that overwhelm you, frighten you that cause you to lose hope and maybe even cause your faith to waiver? We have all gone through or will go through some traumatic "Storm" in our lives that shakes us to our very core. So bad at times, that we aren't sure if we can make it through at all. I have been there multiple times in my life- before and after I gave my life to the Lord. And trust me when I tell you that I NEVER want to do it again without the Lord by my side! Without him I had no hope, no one to trust, to talk to or console me. It was the hardest times of my life being totally alone. I honestly don't know how I lived without God in my life and how anyone would ever want to!

The storms after I surrendered my life to him were still hard but the one thing I always knew for sure was that I was NEVER EVER ALONE! He was then and will always be my hope, my anchor and my peace in my life. No matter what this old world throws at me.

He will be there to catch me when I fall, love me when I feel unlovable and my help in my time of need. What an awesome, loving God we serve and I'm so very proud to be called a child of the king!!

2 Corinthians 4:8-9 ESV
  We are afflicted in every way, but not crushed; perplexed, but not driven to despair; persecuted, but not forsaken; struck down, but not destroyed.

Isaiah 43:1-2 ESV
  But now thus says the Lord, he who created you, 0 Jacob, he who formed you, O Israel: "Fear not, for I have redeemed you; I have called you by name, you are mine. When you pass through the waters, I will be with you; and through the rivers, they shall not overwhelm you; when you walk through fire you shall not be burned, and the flame shall not consume you.

Word of the Day - Sovereign

Sovereign—possessing supreme or ultimate power... absolute, boundless, and unconditional. The way I like to express it is simply to say "God is in control"! He has no limitations! God can do all things and accomplish all things. He has our future planned and already knows what's going to happen in my life, you're like and throughout the world. I bow my life before him in honor and praise as he rules the world in love!

1 Chronicles 29:11
   Yours, O LORD, is the greatness and the power and the glory and the victory and the majesty, indeed everything that is in the heavens and the earth; yours is the dominion, O LORD, and you exalt yourself as head over all...

Nehemiah 9:6
   You alone are the LORD you have made the heavens, The heaven of heavens with all their host, the earth and all that is on it, The seas and all that is in them You give life to all of them and the heavenly host bows down before you.

Word of the Day - Speak up!

So much pain and suffering in this crazy chaotic world we live in. The elderly being neglected and abused, children being left alone to fend for themselves while so called parents "Do their thing", War veterans being pushed aside and treated with disrespect and dishonor, police officers being harassed and sometimes arrested for just doing their jobs, single moms and dads raising children working 2-3 jobs to make ends meet, animals being abused and left in a ditch to die. Who speaks up for them? Who goes one step further to help them and make sure they get what they need? In this "All about me" society we live in where God has been taken out of everything, we need to remember to take care of Gods children who are unable to do so themselves. Pay it forward as everyone says is a great example of speaking out. Sometimes no words are needed to show love, compassion and mercy. Look around, really SEE the people around you. Find out what they need to just survive. Give a hug or smile to someone you meet today. Show Gods love through your words actions and stand up and speak out for those in need. You just never know in doing so when you just might be entertaining angels instead.

Luke 6:31 New International Version (NIV)
  31 Do to others as you would have them do to you.

Proverbs 31:8-9 New International Version (NIV)
  8 Speak up for those who cannot speak for themselves, for the rights of all who are destitute? 9Speak up and judge fairly; defend the rights of the poor and needy

Judy Arnold

Word of the Day -Strength.

Strength, something we all need at one time or another. Without God and the strength he alone gives us, we wouldn't make it through most hardships. Strength- to fight cancer Strength- to make it through a loss of a spouse, child, family member or your best friend Strength- at the loss of your job, your home or your health. To wake up and make it through another day... When it's the last thing you want to do. Our strength comes from the one who walked on water, that calms a raging sea, that put all the stars in the sky, the way maker, the King of Kings!

Isaiah 40:29
  29 He gives strength to the weary and increases the power of the weak.
And my favorite one...

Psalm 40:31
  31 but those who hope in the LORD will renew their strength. They will soar on wings like eagles; they will run and not grow weary, they will walk and not be faint.

Word of the Day - Stronghold

God is our refuge, our strength, our fortress, our deliverer—our stronghold against anything that comes against us. Our hope in every situation and our very present help in time of need. No weapon formed against us will prosper because Gods protection and grace is always with us. What an awesome thing to realize that the God of universe loves us so much that he goes before us and stands behind us protecting and watching over us as we go about our busy lives. Remember today as you worship him and hear his word that the God of Angel Armies is always by your side!!

Psalm 18:2
 The LORD is my rock and my fortress and my deliverer, My God, my rock, in whom I take refuge; My shield and the horn of my salvation, my stronghold.

Nahum 1:7
 The LORD is good, a stronghold in the day of trouble, And He knows those who take refuge in Him.

Judy Arnold

Word of the Day - Strong in the Lord

Every Time I read Scriptures on the armor of God I'm humbled how much He must love his children. He gives us a piece of armor to protect us in every way so that we can stand firm against anything Satan and his demons throw at us. Nothing can penetrate Gods protection, his mighty power!

The Armor- the belt of truth- the body armor of Gods righteousness for your feet, put on the shoes of the gospel of peace- The Breastplate of righteousness- The shield of faith — to withstand the fiery darts of Satan thrown at us. The helmet of salvation and the Sword of the spirit which is the word of God.

He protects us, loves us, forgives us, heals us, and gives us his power, to withstand the evil of this world and will bring us home one day to spend eternity with him! What a glorious time that will be! Be strong in The Lord through his power and might!!! Love and blessings to you all!!

Proverbs 18:1
  The name of the Lord is a strong tower; the righteous run into it and are safe.

Nehemiah 8:10
  Do not grieve, for the joy of the Lord is your strength.

Living God's Word... One Scripture at a Time

Word of the Day - Strong and Courageous

Just how God made us to be! We have strength, endurance, fortitude and safety in the Lord for he goes with us in every battle. Every situation we face we need to remember that God is walking beside us, protecting us in everything we do. Having faith and courage is all about trusting God. Our pastor preached about that in church Sunday. Every decision we make we should take before God trusting him to show us the right way and right thing to do.

How many times do we make a decision within ourselves because it feels right or because it's really what we want to do? Then it goes horrible wrong and we blame God. Did you ask him, did you go to him in prayer and seek His wisdom and counsel? Probably not. I've done it so many times thinking I can do this on my own but it ended up a big mistake.

Courage to trust God and strength to do his will comes from a surrendered heart- sold out to God knowing he only has our best interest at heart. Courage- : mental or moral strength to venture, persevere, and withstand danger, fear, or Difficulty. Strength-something that is regarded as being beneficial or a source of power: I love that song... we were made to be courageous, it's so very true. If you haven't seen the movie courageous you need to watch it. It will bless you so much!

With A mighty God that goes before us and orders our steps. We have the courage and strength to withstand anything this world puts in our path. So be strong in the Lord and have the courage to step out in faith in everything you do trusting the Lord until the He returns one glorious day to bring us home!!!

Deuteronomy 31:6
  Be strong and of good courage, do not fear nor be afraid of them; for the LORD your God, He is the One who goes with you. He will not leave you nor forsake you.

Psalm 27:1

The LORD is my light and my salvation; whom shall I fear? The LORD is the strength of my life; of whom shall I be afraid?

Living God's Word... One Scripture at a Time

Word of the Day - Submit, Resist, Draw Near, Purify, Humble,

Gosh this is a loaded Scripture with so many instructions from God I couldn't pick one word. They all are important... SUBMIT- It is a process surrendering our own will to that of our Father's. RESIST— Resistance can be a defensive maneuver on our part, such as resisting or withstanding the temptation to sin. DRAW NEAR— Drawing near to God is spending time with Him, worshiping Him, praying and talking to Him, inviting Him into every aspect of our lives. Purify—the idea here is to completely turn from our sin, to resolve that we will serve God, and to begin again. That is what true repentance is. HUMBLE... All of us sin and fall short of the glory of God.

However, too few of us have a routine practice of rigorous self—honesty examination. Weekly, even Daily, review of our hearts and behaviors, coupled with confession to God, is an essential practice of humility.(Billy Graham) All these things are important to God yet He makes it so simple. My favorite verse I tell people when I'm asked what God wants us to do is Micah 6:8. He has told you, 0 man, what is good; and what does the Lord require of you but to do justice, and to love kindness, and to walk humbly with your God? Have a blessed day!!

James 4:7-10 New International Version (NIV)
7 Submit yourselves, then, to God. Resist the devil, and he will flee from you. 8 Come near to God and he will come near to you. Wash your hands, you sinners, and purify your hearts, you double—minded. 9 Grieve, mourn and wall. Change your laughter to mourning and your joy to gloom. '10 humble yourselves before the Lord, and he will lift you up.

Judy Arnold

Word of the Day: The Lord-My peace, my strength... My everything!!!

As I read these Scriptures of David singing to the Lord praises of the many things God did for him and the faith and gratitude of his words, it makes me think of all the miracles in my life. All the things big and small that he has done for me and realizing I would have never made it through this far without him in my life. Even when I look back before I was saved I see Him watching over me and keeping me safe. When I was still a sinner he loved me and protected me. It brings me to tears and I know in my heart I never ever want to be without him. Anything this world has to offer can never compare to the perfect peace and strength his love and presence in my life gives me. We never praise him or thank his enough for his faithfulness, forgiveness, grace, mercy and unconditional love that is given freely to us daily. People say being a Christian is hard and costs too much to give up their life or freedom but I'm here to tell them that life without the Lord is empty, without true joy and gives you nothing in the end but hopelessness .Only in Him is true joy, peace, love and to be truly free and have eternity in heaven. I'm so blessed to call him Lord and await the day he calls me home to spend forever in the arms of a loving savior....

Psalm 18:1-6English Standard Version (ESV)
The Lord Is My Rock and My Fortress
To the choirmaster. A Psalm of David, the servant of the Lord, who addressed the words of this song to the Lord on the day when the Lord delivered him from the hand of all his enemies, and from the hand of Saul. He said: 1 I love you, O Lord, my strength. 2 The Lord is my rock and my fortress and my deliverer, my God, my rock, in whom I take refuge, my shield, and the horn of my salvation, my stronghold. 3 I call upon the Lord, who is worthy to be praised, and I am saved from my enemies. 4 The cords of death encompassed me; the torrents of destruction assailed me; 5 the cords of Sheol entangled me; the shares of death confronted me. 6 In my distress I called upon the

Lord; to my God I cried for help. From his temple he heard my voice, and my cry to him reached his ears.

Judy Arnold

Word of the Day - The Spoken Word

The spoken word, how powerful it is! Jesus "spoke" to the fig tree and it withered and died. He tells us in this Scripture that we can move mountains by speaking to them but it's not just the words but the faith to believe it will happen. What are the mountains or problems in your life that are stopping you from receiving all that God has for you? He also tells us to pray and in believing you will receive it. Do you speak to your mountains, your problems and BELIEVE in faith you will receive it? Prayer is an awesome thing but you have to have faith too. I've heard so many sermons about the power of the tongue and what we speak into our lives. I'm always correcting my kids about what they speak out of the mouth. We should be careful about speaking negative things in our life. When things go bad and we get down we say things Like- I will never get a good job or I will never amount to anything or nothing good ever happens in my life. Our faith wavers and we open a door for Satan to come in and use those very statements to work evil in our lives! If words have power, that means everything you say is shaping your life. You may not feel it or see it the minute you speak it, but those words are planting seeds. Because words have power, we clearly have to be intentional with what we speak. Our words should demonstrate the power of God's grace and the Indwelling of the Holy Spirit in our lives

Isaiah 26:1-8 English Standard Version (ESV)
You Keep Him in Perfect Peace
26 In that day this song will be sung in the land of Judah: "We have a strong city; he sets up salvation as walls and bulwarks. 2 Open the gates, that the righteous nation that keeps faith may enter in. 3 you keep him in perfect peace whose mind is stayed on you, because he trusts in you. 4 Trust in the Lord forever, for the Lord God is an everlasting rock. 5 For he has humbled the inhabitants of the height, the lofty city. He lays it low, lays it low to the ground, and casts it to the dust. 6 The foot tramples it, the feet of the poor, the steps of the needy." 7 The path of the

righteous is level; you make level the way of the righteous. 8 In the path of your judgments, O Lord, we wait for you; your name and remembrance are the desire of our soul.

Matthew 21:19-22 New International Version (NIV)
19 Seeing a fig tree by the road, he went up to it but found nothing on it except leaves. Then he said to It, "May you never bear fruit again!" Immediately the tree withered. 20 When the disciples saw this, they were amazed. "How did the fig tree wither so quickly?" they asked. 21 Jesus replied, "Truly I tell you, if you have faith and do not doubt, not only can you do what was done to the fig tree, but also you can say to this mountain, 'Go, throw yourself into the sea,' and it will be done.22 if you believe, you will receive whatever you ask for in prayer."

Word of the Day - The Way, The Truth and The Life!!!

The Word, Jesus! The only way to the Father! The Holy One of God! God gives us a choice of life or death, to live for him or in the world. That free will thing that gets so many us in trouble. But God wants us to live for him of our own choice. He gave us Jesus, the light of the world to shine through the darkness! God wants life for us, abundant joyful life here on earth. By living his word and having a loving relationship with him, our eternity in heaven is guaranteed! Thank him for loving us so much and giving us the ultimate gift through Jesus—salvation!!!

Deuteronomy 30:19:
> ''I call heaven and earth to record this day against you, which I have set before your life and death, blessing and cursing: therefore choose life that both thou and thy seed may live.''

John 8:12 ESV
> Again Jesus spoke to them, saying, ''I am the light of the world. Whoever follows me will not walk in darkness, but will have the light of life

Word of the Day - : The Lamb of God!

Jesus, the Lamb of God, the perfect and ultimate sacrifice for sin. Our Savior and redeemer who gave his life for a sinner like me. As I look at that precious baby lying in a manager, the image of the cross is in my Mind's eye. It humbles me knowing that his life was given for me so I would be forgiven and righteous in My Fathers eyes. The Lamb that was slain, a man that felt every cut of the whip they beat him with, every thorn from the crown they shoved down on his head, the pounding of the nails in his hands-indescribable pain he suffered for us. It's hard to comprehend that kind of unconditional love and sacrifice yet Jesus did that for you and me. I've watched the passion multiple times but when they nailed Jesus to the cross I had to cover my ears and hide my face because the sound penetrated my soul. I just can't of Kings that conquered death and rose again, that every kneel will bow to and every tongue will confess that HE IS LORD!!

Revelation 17:14 New International Version (NIV)
14 They will wage war against the Lamb, but the Lamb will triumph over them because he is Lord of lords and King of kings - and with him will be his called, chosen and faithful followers."

John 1:29
"Behold the Lamb of God who takes away the sins of the world.

Judy Arnold

Word of the Day--The Whole will or "Counsel" of God

In this Scripture Paul tells us, using himself as an example to show us what we are supposed to do as Christians. Our mission field, while we are here is to spread the good news of the gospel- every part of it. I hear so many "feel good" preachers I call them, talk about salvation and how just saying a prayer, helping people and just being good will get you to heaven. They leave out the part they think people don't want to hear but it's the most important part. Repentance and faith! Works alone won't get you to heaven but they don't want to offend anyone. They are doing people such an injustice and putting them in danger of losing eternity in heaven. The WHOLE gospel needs to be told and as sons and daughters of the king, we need to tell everyone we meet about Gods "whole" will for our lives here on earth. Some people will laugh at you or make fun of you. Some will call you crazy and some might even walk away from you but those things shouldn't dissuade you. They need to know the whole truth, the whole gospel and the whole will of God!! Works are good but repentance and faith, believing in Jesus and his true salvation is the only way! So let's get out into the mission field, and let the Holy Spirit guide us as we spread the gospel and help bring souls into the kingdom. Time is short and we need to get on fire for the Lord!! Have a blessed day and week!!

Acts 20:25-28 New International Version (NIV)
25 "Now I know that none of you among whom I have gone about preaching the kingdom will ever see me again. 26 Therefore, I declare to you today that I am innocent of the blood of any of you. 27 For I have not hesitated to proclaim to you the whole will of God. 28 Keep watch over yourselves and all the flock of which the Holy Spirit has made you overseers. Be shepherds of the church of God, which he bought with his own blood.

Word of the Day - Transcendent and Wise

Transcendent— spiritual, divine, exceptional Wise-having or showing experience, knowledge, and good judgment.

Our Lord who created the heavens and the earth, who is above all things seeks to have a relationship with us- his creation made in his image. The Lord Almighty, El Shaddai the one who is great and greatly to be praised. One day we will look upon his face and walk and talk with him like Adam and eve did. I can't begin to imagine or comprehend that but just being in his presence here on earth gives me peace beyond my understanding.

In his infinite wisdom and his desire to have a personal relationship with us, he sent Jesus to die for our sins and to put us back in right relationship with him. Choose to serve him, surrender your life and everything within you to him. The joy, peace and love you receive in doing this changes your life forever and gives you a hope of eternity with our Lord!

John 1:29 New International Version (NIV)
John Testifies About Jesus
29 The next day John saw Jesus coming toward him and said, "Look, the Lamb of God, who takes away the sin of the world.

Isaiah 55:19
"For as the heavens are higher than the earth, so are my ways higher than your ways and my thoughts than your thoughts."

Judy Arnold

Word of the Day Truthful and Wickedness (evil)

These are two words that are as opposite as black and white, good and bad, right and wrong. Have you considered which one people think or say you are? So many people that I'm blessed to share the word with always say pretty much the same thing when I ask do you have a personal relationship with Jesus. Their response is, well I believe there is a God and then "I'm a good person. But the fruit of their life shows a totally different thing.

"Wickedness" a word not heard or used much these days but is the same thing as evil. The world tells us it's ok to be "yourself" that it's "ok" to do your thing and everything will be alright...but that is so far from the truth!!!! Evil is evil and truth is truth- there is no getting around that. There is no gray area in the word of God but the world's current view revolves around it's all about me mentality! It's all about Jesus-the way, the truth and the life!!

We strive to live as he did in truth and love, forgiving all and resisting evil. When in doubt about how to live your life and what is acceptable to the Lord, look to one that walked among sin and the wickedness on the earth yet knew no sin, our perfect savior!!!

Proverbs 12: 1-3 New International Version (NIV)
12 Whoever loves discipline loves knowledge, but whoever hates correction is stupid. 2 Good people obtain favor from the Lord, but he condemns those who devise wicked schemes. 3 No one can be established through wickedness, but the righteous cannot be uprooted.

Proverbs 12:19-20 New International Version (NIV)
19 Truthful lips endure forever, but a lying tongue lasts only a moment. 20 Deceit is in the hearts of those who plot evil, but those who promote peace have joy.

Living God's Word... One Scripture at a Time

Word of the Day: The Name of God!

I so love talking about the many names of God because it reminds me of how he is everything in my life! But Jehovah Jireh - our provider- pretty much describes it. Everything we need in this life he takes care of before we even ask. He goes before us and makes a way! He loves us sooo much they he cares about the smallest things that matters to us. An example that will make you Laugh. I'm horrible about losing my glasses. I have like 4 pair around the house but somehow manage to misplace all of them. One day I was frustrated and said, Lord, please help me find at least one pair! I heard a quiet voice gently Say, look on your head!!! Oh my gosh! I laughed so hard and said. Duh. Thank you Lord!! Yes he has a sense of humor too and that's another reason I love him so much.

Yahweh - our God, our healer, our provider and our very present help in time of need! Whatever you are going through, whatever you need, look to the one who made the universe, set the stars in the sky, who cares about every single thing in our life - our God, Yahweh! Jehovah Jireh - our everything

Acts 4:12 ESV
 And there is salvation in no one else, for there is no other name under heaven given among men by which we must be saved.

Proverbs 18:10 ESV
 The name of the LORD is a strong tower; the righteous man runs into it and is safe.

Judy Arnold

Word of the Day - Unto the Lord"

Everything we do, say, act and treat people should glorify God in some way, shape or form. Your "witness" to your family, friends, co- workers and every one you meet should be pleasing to the Lord. This Scripture says to use wisdom and grace in teaching or telling people about the Lord. To let his light shine through you in everything you do. Wives submitting to their husbands as you do to the Lord, treating them with respect as the spiritual head of the household "Honor your father and mother" - which is the first commandment with a promise - "so that it may go well with you and that you may enjoy long life on the earth."... We should use God as an example of how we treat each other and our family members. If we love as Christ loves, forgive as Christ does, be merciful as Christ does then joy and peace will reign in your life, your marriage and your home!

Colossians 3:16-21 King James Version (KJV)
16 Let the word of Christ dwell in you richly in all wisdom; teaching and admonishing one another in psalms and hymns and spiritual songs, singing with grace in your hearts to the Lord. 17 And whatsoever ye do in word or deed, do all in the name of the Lord Jesus, giving thanks to God and the Father by him. 18 Wives, submit yourselves unto your own husbands, as it is fit in the Lord. 19 Husbands, love your wives, and be not bitter against them. 20 Children, obey your parents in all things: for this is well pleasing unto the Lord. 21 Fathers, provoke not your children to anger, lest they be discouraged.22 Wives, submit yourselves to your own husbands as you do to the Lord. 23 For the husband is the head of the wife as Christ is the head of the church, his body, of which he is the Savior. Husbands loving their wives as Christ loves the church and know their worth is more precious than rubies

Ephesians 6:2-3 "Honor your father and mother" - which is the first commandment with a promise - 3 "so that it may go well with you and that you may enjoy long life on the earth."

Numbers 6:24-26 New International Version (NIV)
24 The Lord bless you and keep you; 25 The Lord make His face shine upon you, and be gracious to you; 26 The Lord lift up His countenance upon you, And give you peace.'"

Judy Arnold

Word of the Day - Unconditional

God's love for us is unconditional, unchangeable, and everlasting. What a loving God we have that loves us much that he sacrificed his only son so that our sins could be forgiven and we could be free!! That's real love from an awesome God! Spend time with him today and thank him for a love compared to no other that he freely gives to those who seek him. Hugs to all and hope your weekend is full of peace and joy in the Lord.

Nehemiah 9:71
  But you are a forgiving God, gracious and compassionate, slow to anger and abounding in love...

1 John 3:1
  "How great is the love the Father has lavished on us, that we should be called children of the King.

Word of the Day - Walk Humbly Before God

As I read this Scripture it brings to mind a question that is asked so many times by Christians in their walk with God. What does God expect of me or what does God want me to do? I don't really understand why when everything we need to know is in the Bible. God has given us a guideline to follow- a rule book if you will of how to live holy and righteous. A world of knowledge in His word and we need to spend more time reading and understanding it instead of phones, computers, iPod, television and all the things that distract us from spending time with God.

Not that there is anything wrong with any of that but when it becomes an obsession taking up all your time and attention and you have no extra time for God then it becomes a problem. All of the things mentioned in this Scripture...compassion, kindness, humility, gentleness, patience, forgiveness all revolve around one thing— love. If we love our neighbors as our self, and love God with all our heart, soul and mind then we walk in true love, true humility and in perfect peace. I leave you with one of my favorite Scriptures.

Colossians 3:12-17 New International Version (NIV)
12 Therefore, as God's chosen people, holy and dearly loved, clothe yourselves with compassion, kindness, humility, gentleness and patience. 13 Bear with each other and forgive one another if any of you has a grievance against someone. Forgive as the Lord forgave you. 14 And over all these virtues put on love, which binds them all together in perfect unity. 15 Let the peace of Christ rule in your hearts, since as members of one body you were called to peace. And be thankful. 16 Let the message of Christ dwell among you richly as you teach and admonish one another with all wisdom through psalms, hymns, and songs from the Spirit, singing to God with gratitude in your hearts. 17 And whatever you do, whether in word or deed, do it all in the name of the Lord Jesus, giving thanks to God the Father through him.

Micah 6:8 New International Version

He has shown you, O mortal, what is good. And what does the LORD require of you? To act justly and to love mercy and to walk humbly with your God.

Word of the Day-Witness

Being a witness for the Lord is one of the greatest most powerful works we can do. So many times I have wanted to witness to a friend or loved one but that old liar" fear"creeped in. Satan is good at his job of instilling that in us especially when it comes to sharing Jesus with someone. He sits on your shoulder spilling lie after lie about how you aren't good enough or holy enough to be a "real" witness. He reminds you of all your mistakes and why no one would listen to you. Then fear sets in and we walk away, losing maybe the only opportunity we had to tell that one person that really needed to hear about the Lord!
But when we are filled with Holy Ghost power NOTHING can stand in our way! He gives us the secure ability to know who we are in Christ and to punch through that wall of fear Satan has built up. Then our God nature shines through with Holy Ghost power and the exact words that person needs to hear spills out. That's when you know that you know that he is working through you and with you. Don't be afraid to spread the word and witness about Jesus, his awesome salvation plan and what a loving savior he is. Let your light shine through the darkness and tell everyone that Jesus is Lord!!! Hugs and blessings everyone

Acts 1:7-8 New International Version (NIV)

7 He said to them: "It is not for you to know the times or dates the Father has set by his own authority. 8 But you will receive power when the Holy Spirit comes on you; and you will be my witnesses in Jerusalem, and in all Judea and Samaria, and to the ends of the earth

Judy Arnold

Word of the Day - Victorious

Victory in Jesus—a statement with three simple words. We struggle so much in our daily lives fighting against things we have no control over. We try and try until we are at our wits end, tired and beaten down. Then as a last resort, we turn to God begging him to fix the mess we are in. The word says the battle is the Lords and yet we don't trust him enough to let him take control when a problem first arises. As the word says... in this world you will have troubles but don't worry.

Jesus has overcome the world! That means there is nothing he can't do but we have to lay it at his feet. We have to give him total control and trust him with all our heart! We make mistakes, do the wrong thing and get ourselves in real messes sometimes but the good news is God always makes a way and gives us victory! We can't do anything within ourselves but with Christ, ALL things are possible! I leave you with the lyrics of this old church hymn that still rings as true today as it did back then...

I heard an old, old story,
How a Savior came from glory,
How He gave His life on Calvary
To save a wretch like me;
I heard about His groaning,
Of His precious blood's atoning, Then I repented of my sins And won the victory.
Chorus
0 victory in Jesus, My Savior, forever.
He sought me and bought me
With His redeeming blood;
He loved me ere I knew Him
And all my love is due Him,
He plunged me to victory, beneath the cleansing flood.

1 John 5:4 ESV

For everyone who has been born of God overcomes the world. And this is the victory that has overcome the world—our faith.

1 Corinthians 10:13

13 No temptation has overtaken you except what is common to mankind. And God is faithful; he will not let you be tempted beyond what you can bear. But when you are tempted, he will also provide a way out so that you can endure it.

Judy Arnold

Word of the Day - Yielding to God

What does it mean to you to really Yield to God? I have had so many people say to me: I am good person. That is a good thing but what does God say about you? To yield to God is to give your whole life to him, to keep your body pure, keep his commandments, and by doing his will. I always "bounce" every decision, everything I do off what the word says.

You will never go wrong that way. I use to make decisions and do things based on my emotions or feelings but they always ended up going wrong. I couldn't figure out why I couldn't do anything right, in my job, my family life or my relationships. I went from one disaster to another, always feeling like I had an empty whole in my being that nothing could fill. It was a horrible feeling and I was going nowhere fast. But when I finally realized through counseling and tons of prayers from family and friends that I needed to fill that hole with Jesus! I yielded to him in every way and all I can say now is I wish I wouldn't have waited so long!!! I lost years and experienced a lot of sadness and heartbreak. The good news is...l have victory in every aspect of my life all because of him!

Romans 12:1-2
> I appeal to you therefore, brothers, by the mercies of God, to present your bodies as a living sacrifice, holy and acceptable to God, which is your spiritual worship. Do not be conformed to this world, but be transformed by the renewal of your mind, that by testing you may discern what the will of God is, what is good and acceptable and perfect.

John 14:15
> If you love me, you will keep my commandments.

Judy Arnold

Earthly Stories with a Heavenly Meaning